TIME MANAGEMENT FOR ACADEMICS

Time Management For Academics

Harry Lewis and Philip Hills

Peter Francis Publishers

Peter Francis Publishers
The Old School House
Little Fransham
Dereham
Norfolk NR19 2JP
UK

A CIP catalogue record for this book
is available from the British Library

ISBN 1-870167-32-5

Printed and bound in Great Britain by Biddles Ltd,
Guildford and King's Lynn.

Table of Contents

About the Authors

Dr Harry Lewis is a Senior Lecturer in Philosophy at the University of Leeds. In addition to pursuing a career in teaching and research, with a special interest in the philosophy of mind, he has a wide administrative experience, including periods as faculty sub-dean and as head of his department. He has also served as President of the Association of University Teachers, Leeds Local Association. He has experience of database development maintaining an interest in the application of information technology to university administration, and has been active in promoting the use of workload allocation systems in the university workplace.

Dr Philip Hills is Head of the Centre for Research into Human Communication and Learning based in Cambridge. He is also a visiting lecturer in universities across the UK working in partnership with staff development on research related topics. He has experience of developing teaching and learning systems, is author/editor of over seventy books and many papers in the field of education, communication skills and information technology.

Preface

This is a book for academic staff at all levels. Since it is intended to help you with your time management problems we have written it to be used in any of three main ways:

(1) by reading it in sequence – beginning at Chapter 1 and reading straight through to Chapter 11;

(2) as a resource-book and reference; (if you are in urgent need of help in a particular area, turn to the index or the extended table of contents and go directly to our discussion of your chosen area);

(3) as a self-teaching course of five modules with a short research project whose successful completion leads to the 'degree of Master of Time'. (We explain this further in Chapter 1.)

Both of us have been interested in the subject of time and its management for many years and by chance came together at a time of considerable changes in the academic environment when we both wanted to do something to help academics cope with these changes. This book and 'course' is the result. The final version has been long in the making but it is itself an illustration that if one has a goal and the will to pursue it, mountains can be moved.

Like any course this one can be improved and we would welcome feedback from those who pursue the course to its end, with ideas for revisions.

Harry Lewis and Philip Hills

1 Introduction

You may ask:

Why should I be concerned with mastering time?

Our answer:

- To become more effective

- To enjoy a sense of mastery

- To be able to control a situation, and not to let it control you

'Time management' is the control or management of activity in relation to various time-related factors: the passage of time itself, deadlines, and the natural rhythms of life. The control and co-ordination of people's use of time has been a pervasive feature of work in industrialized societies since the eighteenth century. The development of time-keeping techniques and the character of work are closely related. In schools and universities, teaching activity is governed by published timetables: a weekly timetable of classes, and an annual timetable of terms or semesters, and examination periods.

The contemporary concern for time management has arisen within the last thirty years with a principal focus on the middle-ranking or senior executive in industry or commerce. Concern for time management has now invaded universities, as a result of two factors: one, the development of staff training courses that have introduced 'managerial' skills to academic staff; and, two, the increases in workloads placed upon individuals as a result of a variety of changes in universities which are discussed in Chapter 2.

The expression 'time management' is itself a recent coinage but has gained general currency since the early 1980s. As our own brief explanation above reveals, it is not the happiest of terms to express the intended meaning. Time is a dimension that, as such, cannot be influenced or 'managed'. But metaphors extending 'time' beyond the dimensional are commonplace. It would not only be difficult but also pointless to attempt to give a single account of all these usages.

Why do we choose the word 'management'? This is another item of contemporary jargon (not to say: 'management-speak'). The connotation it has in our title phrase is the same as it has in the phrase 'self-management' when it is contrasted with 'self-control': it reflects a view that one's own activity, like that of a manager's subordinates, can be influenced but may not be tightly controlled. Two semantic threads are entwined together: one reflecting views about organizations and working groups; the other, an analogy between individual and group that is at least as old as Plato. To speak of 'managing' others' activity reflects a perception that human behaviour is a somewhat wayward product of external and internal influences, that we can hope to influence but not to command absolutely. 'Command and control' in an organization was supposedly tight and mechanical; 'management' is more sensitive to the character and wishes of subordinates, as well as to influences in the environment. 'Will-power' in an individual was conceived as an iron rule of the 'subordinate' parts of the personality by an internal tyrant, the 'Will'. Both individual psychology and the understanding of behaviour in organizations have moved on, so now we have 'self-management' in place of 'will-power'. And so we have also 'time management', which can be interpreted as 'self-management in relation to time'.

The phrase 'time management' has become part of the language. We trust that our own use of it will not cause confusion. However we may express the point, what we know we can do is to modify our own time-consuming activity so as to achieve more within a given time.

We hope that this book will revive your enthusiasm for your life and your work. It is good to remember one important principle:

> Breaking out of our present time management problems is as much to do with intervening in the onward rush of events, which have a momentum largely, but not wholly, outside our control, as with changing our own behaviour.

If you are in the middle of a stampeding herd, it is not easy, nor is it wise, to stop suddenly – you could just get trampled under foot. The external processes in which we are enmeshed have a momentum of their own that we need to respect, even though we also need to influence them.

Do not try to change everything at once. You should look at time management as a voyage of exploration; as a research project which you can undertake for yourself – and without additional funding!

One of the possible uses of our book is to enable you to pursue your own study for the 'degree of Master of Time', and to this end we have suggested a course for you to pursue. This 'course' consists of five modules including a short research project, suggestions for tackling specific problems, and a 'self-examination'.

The syllabus for the course is as follows:

Module 1   Read Chapter 2.

This will orient you to the external factors that are impinging on us.

Module 2   Read Chapter 3.

This chapter gives you a framework for gaining self-knowledge relevant to your own situation.

Module 3   Read Chapters 4, 5 and 6.

These chapters deal with three subjects, which we list as our three major tasks in university work: teaching, research, administration. Begin to observe your situation to provide data for your later research project. Use the content of these chapters to improve your data and approach.

Module 4   Read Chapters 8, 9 and 10.

Read these chapters on paperwork, working with other people, and tackling the problem at its source. Apply the principles from these chapters to the three main areas of activity which are discussed in Chapters 4 to 6.

Module 5   Read Chapter 7. (Research project)

> Select an area of your work for special attention, and apply the course of action described in this chapter to it. Review progress against the list of characteristics of the 'Master of Time' listed at the end of this chapter.

Chapter 11 is both a summary and an aide-mémoire for you, stressing the most important points in previous chapters and extending them with some conventional time management wisdom.

When you have completed this chapter you will have assessed yourself against the criteria for the 'award of a Master of Time'. You should then not only be more proficient in your use of time but should be able to go forward as a researcher to refine and improve your time management techniques.

2 The World We Struggle in

This chapter reviews the external factors which shape our environment and reflects on the ways in which our activities as individuals are influenced by them.

When you have read this chapter you will:

(1) have reviewed ten major factors shaping the present university environment;

(2) have considered the difference between changes which are qualitative and quantitative;

(3) recognize the unique role of individual academics and the pressures upon them.

Influencing factors

Time management does not take place in a vacuum. It involves not only individual people but also their colleagues at work, and their family and companions outside work. It involves the various frameworks afforded by their departments and the larger institutions in which they in turn are set. It involves the environment of the organization and of the individual academic: the sources, however far-flung and remote from today's tasks, and the ultimate destinations, of the students and the research projects with which we are involved. The challenges we face as individuals are powerfully shaped

Expansion of the university system
Funding
Staff recruitment
Students
Teaching methods
Subject content
Assessment
Research and teaching
Publication
Administration

Figure 2.1: Factors shaping our environment

by these external factors. In this chapter we review some of these factors (see Figure 2.1) and reflect on the ways in which our activity as individuals is influenced by them. In Chapter 3 we shall consider in what ways we are able to respond to these; but first in this chapter let us examine each of these factors in turn.

Expansion of the university system

In the past fifty years the university system has expanded dramatically in size, and has witnessed development from an 'élite' to a mass system, through the expansion of existing institutions, the creation of new universities on green field sites, and the enhancement and development of what were previously non-university institutions.

The increase in teaching activity meets the needs of a student body that has grown in response to increased 'participation rates' among young adults entering university immediately after completion of school education, and among other adult groups.

Funding

The costs of university education – tuition and living costs – are borne variously by the students (during their studies and after graduation), their families, and by governments, with some contributions from sponsoring employers, charitable institutions and other sources. In the greater part of the developed world, the public purse has been the dominant source of university funding, with the students and their families playing the other major role.

Unfortunately, the funds which are available to pay for university education have not risen in proportion to the expansion in student numbers. Funding indeed *per student* has been progressively reduced, especially so in those universities and university systems that depend on a public purse.

Funding for research is earmarked for that purpose, and comes from sources different from those that provide the resources for teaching. The research-funding system for universities in the United Kingdom is based on the 'dual' principle, with a formula-based foundation, and a superstructure of individual contracts awarded by government research bodies and by charities and industrial sponsors. The expansion of universities has been accompanied by an expansion in the number of *researchers* although not in a commensurate increase in funds for expensive research activities. The result of this is that some of the most costly forms of research, for example in high-energy physics, finds themselves in a state of continual crisis over their funding.

Staff recruitment

In many countries the past twenty years have seen a succession of stop-go cycles in academic staff recruitment. Reductions in funding have at some periods provoked universities to seek voluntary early retirements and redundancies from amongst their staff; at other periods, student numbers have increased so rapidly that it has been possible to recruit new academic staff in significant numbers, but increasingly to fixed or short-term appointments and with lowered expectations of long-term or 'tenured' academic employment.

The enforced staff reductions, the rapid recruitment, and the higher levels of review entailed by the use of short contracts, have increased the volume of personnel activity undertaken by heads of departments and other senior academic staff. Added to this have been new bureaucratic requirements, often undertaken with good intentions, for example, in the monitoring of equal opportunities in the recruitment and promotion processes. The continual rise of the academic 'quality industry' has been accompanied inevitably (you might say) by an increase in staff development activity, mostly focused on teaching, but also taking into account other new areas of activity, for example, budget management. And so, for many senior academics as well as for newly appointed staff, time has had to be taken out for further training, in addition to the extra time devoted to the recruitment and the monitoring of new staff and (in the periods of 'down-sizing') negotiating over those early retirements and re-deployments (sometimes referred to, euphemistically, as 'restructuring'). For new recruits the academic career has now become much less attractive, as more staff are recruited to fixed-term contracts with reduced prospects of moving to permanent contracts. We have seen that salaries in universities have declined in comparison with those of other professional groups, and yet in contrast to this, workloads have increased for staff at all levels.

Students

The character of the student bodies of universities is continually changing. Expansion and the rising rates of participation in higher education by young people of school-leaving age have seen an increase in the proportion of students (from the home country or state) whose family background does not include university graduates. Changes in approaches to teaching in pre-university educational institutions affect the preparedness of new students for their university courses. Managed funding regimes have driven universities in many countries to recruit ever more aggressively for international students, and the proportion of such students has grown substantially in some departments. In a similar way, the number and proportion of 'mature' students, who come to university later in life, including those who undertake some university study in the context of their main employment, has also increased.

Teaching methods

There is no general worldwide agreement about the methods of teaching used in universities, or about the frameworks and programmes that give structure to the studies for a university degree. Economic pressures, educational re-search, continual self-criticism, have led to an increased pace of change in teaching methods and teaching structures. As paymaster governments and other sponsors seek to reassure themselves that universities are making good use of their funds, external scrutiny of 'quality' in teaching has grown and developed.

It is a commonplace that the pace of technological change accelerated in the late twentieth century, but it is possible to lose sight of the extent and impact of technological change among the dreaming spires of universities. In the same institution the most traditional *teaching* technologies – ancient lecture rooms, talk, with or without chalk; equally ancient tutorial rooms – can still be found alongside the most advanced *research* technologies. Even so teaching technology continues to change, most evidently in the development of computer use within courses, but more humbly in the advance of visual aids of other kinds. In the administration of universities, however, computers came into use as they had done in other organizations, to assist in the management of payrolls and finance, the registration of students, and also in campus-wide and external communications.

Subject content

There is constant change too in the content of the subjects which students learn, and which our research seeks to advance. In all academic disciplines the pace of development has increased. Specialisms have narrowed as the number of workers in a field, the amount of published research, have grown. Where thirty years ago one scholar could read all the publications in his or her chosen discipline and native language, today a single researcher can with difficulty keep up with work in a small sub-area perhaps one-tenth of the size – where too the publications involved will include not only traditional forms of publication in learned journals and books, but also an increasing tide of 'samizdat' publication, pre-prints and electronic outpourings; all this only partly offset by a growth of continually-updated 'secondary' sources: bibliographies, abstracts and specialized review journals.

An element in increased research activity, bound up with the faster pace of subject development, is the continued rise in the number of academic conferences and colloquia. Specialization and fragmentation of disciplines and the development of new inter-disciplinary areas provide the rationale. In some countries the major conferences form an integral part of the staff recruitment system for appointments, especially first appointments, to academic positions. Therefore, an increased number of advanced students help to populate the conferences which provide students of specialized areas with not only the social contact with others of similar interests, but also of finding in these gatherings those opportunities that they need to make contacts with potential employers, and potential publishers of their works. (Publishers' representatives usually attend the larger conferences in order to keep an eye open for developments in the subject as well as to recruit authors – preferably of the sort of textbooks which promise to sell in large numbers.)

Assessment

Marking or grading of students' work is an integral part of academic work; as is editing, selection and refereeing of other scholars' books and articles. In some countries it has also been standard for the examinations of one university to be subject to 'external' scrutiny: examiners are appointed from a second university to assist in the assessment process. Such external examining has become more onerous as external examiners are increasingly cast in the role of inquisitors.

The ever-growing demands of funding agencies, especially governments, for accountability have led to a new development of external 'audits' and 'assessments' of departmental activity in teaching and research (sometimes taken together, sometimes as separate). In the United Kingdom there are now national systems for 'quality' assessment and audit for both teaching and research. These systems entail much paperwork and involve academics in spending new time both as assessors or auditors and as the objects of such scrutiny.

Research and teaching

Research and teaching compete for our time. Some aspects of teaching activity can be timetabled tidily, being predictable some time ahead. We know when our classes are, when our marking will come in. During teaching terms or semesters, research activity has to be fitted around such commitments. (But where research involves laboratory work, that too may need to be planned in advance and fitted in to the diary of several team members.)

In general, research activity is harder to plan and to fit neatly into slots in the working week. Original ideas do not come to order, and we may go through long fallow periods, but also periods where new ideas come quickly and we want to drop all other activities to work out and record our inspirations. Thus not only do research and teaching compete for our time; their natural rhythms are apt to be quite different. Serving these two masters can involve conflicts that are not resolved by 'compartmentalizing' our time into research and teaching periods.

Publication

'Publish or perish' has been the rule for decades in some countries and disciplines, but by now is the standard rather than the exception in all university systems where research is part of the work, as much in the humanities and social sciences as in the mathematical and laboratory sciences and medicine. The performance of individual academics, of departments and of universities is measured in the quantity and the perceived distinction of publications and other research output. (Thus also the number of learned journals has increased apparently without limit; and perforce the number of readers per journal article has fallen – one estimate places the average readership of a published paper at *four*.)

Administration

'Administration' is of such concern to academics that we have dedicated a chapter to it (Chapter 6). The term itself is an 'umbrella-word' that covers just about anything we do not like doing. Form-filling and paperwork, student recruitment activities, arranging and attending meetings, personnel and advice work have a way of demanding time at the most inconvenient moments and of breaking into a chain of thought or a productive supervision session. The work of coping with information overload and bureaucratic interventions, the auditing of accounts, and many other similar activities, conspire to displace time from teaching and research. Their demands often arrive at inconvenient moments and have a way of interrupting us whatever we are doing. These very varied tasks have a rhythm – or rather, an 'arrhythmia' – of their own, so that it is not only a matter of the total demand they make on our time, but also the untidy mess they make of our plans to get ahead with serious academic work.

Heads of departments find themselves answering to university authorities for their colleagues, and being treated as if they were 'in-line' above them. The conflicting expectations of the parties involved, that is, university authorities and colleagues, can readily lead to difficulty.

The mode of uniqueness that we may have in our administrative roles is rather different from that of our research and teaching roles (which are considered further below). The curious ambivalence of our attitude to administration combines a contempt for routine and repetitive work with a wish to ensure that academic decisions, such as those concerning recruitment of students and staff, are made by 'fellows', members of the guild or club, and are not passed to a professional administrator, or a secretary, let alone a computer. The net result of these conflicting attitudes can be that individual academics become vital 'nodes' in a network of decision-making and paper-flows; where if that node does not pass the required decisions or documents to its client nodes, a far wider system is affected – or infected. (We consider these matters further in Chapter 9 when we come to consider working with other people.)

The process of change

The academic, largely autonomous as he or she may be in academic work, participates in processes which are strongly influenced by the sources and eventual destinations of the students they teach; and by the audiences and sponsors of research. The *quantitative* changes are palpable: more students, less money for each student; pressure for more publications, less money for each researcher and each project. These changes have effects on our use of time: we spend more time on teaching, but also more on research, even as we find that each student, and even each paper or article, receives less attention than it would have done ten years previously. Other, *qualitative* changes divert effort from traditional activities. Much new time is spent dancing to the tune of the quality controllers, preparing paperwork, analysing student surveys, filling in assessment forms, and the like. Changes in teaching structures and departmental re-organizations soak up many hours in committee meetings. Figure 2.2 shows the main qualitative and quantitative changes that are taking place.

Implementing changes is costly, whether the impetus for change originates within or outside the unit that is changing. There are hidden costs of change. Individuals who are required to learn new skills lose effectiveness until they have 'got up to speed' with the new systems. This is all the more true when the system involves many people or units, as is commonly the case with teaching structures, departmental re-organizations, or the introduction of new administrative systems. However beautiful the blueprint for the new system, the reality will inevitably involve a period of 'de-skilling' and subsequent painful readjustment. In the short term, there is nothing as efficient as the old system, however inefficient it may seem to the consultants who make a living from recommending changes. As the average life-span of systems shortens, so the proportion of total effort required by adjustment to new systems rises.

Each of the changes we have noted has its cost in effort and time for those involved in it. The working lives of most academics are affected by several of the changes we have just noted. Thus, as we shall consider immediately, the effects of many changes are not only *additive*; there is a

	More	**Less**
Quantitative changes	More students.	Less money/student.
	Pressure for more	Less money for each project
	publication.	and each researcher.
Qualitative changes	Quality control.	
	Paperwork.	
	Analysing student surveys.	
	Filling in assessment forms.	

Figure 2.2: Qualitative and quantitative changes

price we pay that results from the ways in which they compete for our attention and dedication.

Academic life has long involved an element of competition – from competition for high marks and grades in school to competition for research funding and the higher academic honours. But in the later decades of the twentieth century a 'market' approach to public services infected the academic world. Individuals, their departments, and whole institutions are now placed in competition with one another for just about any resource or 'market': *students* (local, from the home country, from overseas); *staff* who will enhance departmental performance against the various external norms; such *grades* as may be awarded to whole departments, including (in the United Kingdom) both teaching and research assessment grades; *research grants*; *publication* in leading refereed journals; and so on.

As governments and some of their voters have become more wary of spending on education, so universities and their staffs have increasingly come into conflict with them. The Dearing report (1997) and the immediate government response to it spelt the end of the regime of 'free' higher education in the United Kingdom. (Under this system, the central government paid the tuition charges for all full-time undergraduate students from within the European Union who attended British universities.)

An unwelcome side-effect of other changes – in resources, in pressures on departments to perform – has been an increase in conflict among colleagues. Resources shrink, demands for 'quality' go up; colleagues whose idiosyncratic ways once seemed lovable or at the least tolerable, are now felt to be a liability unless they 'pull their weight' or modify their teaching or their research style in order to fit the new criteria.

In comparison with people in most other walks of life, including other professions, academics have enjoyed considerable freedom in the organiz-ation of their working lives; and have usually been party to shaping the local structures of teaching and research within which they work. With the new levels of external scrutiny, both financial and performance-related, the centre of control has moved away from the individual academic. Local discretion has been tempered by the need to meet requirements of institutions and of sundry external paymasters and auditors.

Conflict, control, time and stress

What have these conflicts to do with our problems of managing time? In many cases they soak up time. For example, increased competition for research funding from public bodies and other sponsors means that would-be grant holders spend more of their working time in preparing applications that prove unsuccessful. It is where the various pressures lead to interpersonal conflict, that it becomes at once distracting (from other activity) at the expense of overall productivity, and costly in itself as various meetings and appeal procedures are invoked, at least in the more serious cases. Conflicts of loyalties may cause no more than discomfort, or may steal time spent agonizing on difficult decisions.

Workloads are often spoken of as if they were just like any other kinds of *loads*, such as weights applied to a platform, tonnes of traffic borne by a bridge; subject to measurement along one dimension. Excessive workloads are compared to a mass too great for the bridge to bear; and efficiency, or effective time management, becomes a matter of re-designing the bridge to bear a greater weight, but for the same or lower cost.

We must bear in mind that the excessive workloads that fill out all available nooks and crannies of time, and some we would rather not make available – during wakeful nights, or weeks we should rather spend on our shrinking annual leave – involve not just the one, but several dimensions. Time is indeed a single dimension; but the 'loads' that use up our time are of many kinds. Our problems are not readily understood as involving simply a lack of time. Consider the difference between working a series of 80-hour weeks to finish a research project or book which is going well, which you have chosen as your own, and in conditions where you are confident that any other responsibilities can safely wait until the project is complete; and working the same hours but on a mixture of overdue examination marking, urgent and largely unforeseen meetings with colleagues presenting a range of problems they are anxious for you to solve for them, with distraught students who are anxious about their examination results, and on paperwork that is associated with the visit to your department of an official assessment panel.

The problems of *control*, *stress* and *time* are linked together and conspire to affect the quality of our working lives. The research project that is going well may take up much time, but then there you are in control, and the 'stress' involved is positive, the adrenalin flows associated with the excitement of discovery and creation. But using the same time on a mixture of marking, difficult personal interviews, and form-filling for some alien authority whose interference you despise, is far less pleasant partly because of the much lower degree of control you exert over your activity, and also because the stresses involved are of the unpleasant variety. There is guilt at missing deadlines, anger or frustration at demands placed upon one by colleagues and students, fear or profound distaste at having to complete forms for a loathed and interfering external assessment panel who (in your humble opinion) could not manage an academic department to save their lives.

The individual academic

The external pressures and problems that we have mentioned cause difficulties for individual academics in many different ways. But as much as any public performer or creative artist, academics are also driven by pressures from within, from their own commitment to the subject they profess, and their own distinctive academic ambitions.

These days universities have 'mission statements', and they are apt to refer to teaching and research as their 'core business'; so demeaned have we become by management-speak. Whether the matter is expressed thus or in less managerial language, we all know that research and teaching are done by universities only insofar as individual academics engage in these activities. There is indeed collaboration too; for example, it is the norm for research activity in some laboratory sciences. This collaboration is initiated and propelled by the collaborators, not ordained from above by some authority dragooning people into teams. In spite of all the various re-organizations of faculties and departments, it is still the academic disciplines that determine institutional boundaries; and it is to a good department of, for example, chemistry, or history, that the leading or aspiring chemist, or historian, wishes to become attached in their next appointment.

It is the rule rather than the exception for an academic to have a research programme that is uniquely his or her own. Like as not too they will have a unique portfolio of courses for teaching, such that if they were to leave the department, some at least of those courses would cease to exist. We consider administrative roles, and the more elementary levels of teaching, as more 'transferable' among colleagues. But universities – in this respect no different from other large organizations – tend to have dedicated staff who specialize in aspects of administration to the extent that they as individuals become indispensable to the smooth working of the machine they operate.

Thus an academic may be unique in the world in a research area. The pressure that comes from this and the knowledge of it is like that on a creative artist, to complete his or her *oeuvre* at any personal cost, because there will never be another like it.

Many time management manuals include the advice: Do things only 'well enough'. It is in the nature of academic work, as in the nature of international competition in athletics or sport, that the individual always seeks to achieve his or her personal 'best', without consideration of cost. The name of the game is to achieve the Olympic gold medal in one's own special field. In research, 'making do' is not seen as an option. In teaching, where some colleagues approach it as a craft, an engineering discipline where desired standards must be set against resources of time and facilities, others approach it still in the same way as they approach their research, and are disappointed if students' assignments reveal misunderstandings of their insights.

Summary of Chapter 2

This chapter has considered factors which are shaping the university environment, including expansion of the university system, changes in funding, staff recruitment, student recruitment, changes in teaching methods and subject content, assessment, research and teaching, publication pressures and increasing administration. Costs in effort and time have been considered in terms of the mounting pressures. The uniqueness of the individual academic in their field has been considered.

3 Breaking Out

This chapter looks at the way you cope with the factors impinging on you. It gives a framework for action to take control of your time, a framework which is further developed in the following three chapters.

When you have read this chapter you will:

(1) have considered a nine-step plan for tackling your time management problems;

(2) know the importance of sustaining and improving your performance;

(3) have begun to investigate the process through a course of study leading to the 'award of Master of Time'.

In this chapter we move from our survey of large-scale factors to a consideration of a person-sized problem. The first conundrum that faces anyone who is hoping to gain more control over their use of time is: How do you ever get started? If you are running to stay in the same place, if new demands are piling up faster than you can deal with old ones, if as soon as you settle down to catch up with a backlog of paperwork the telephone rings, or someone knocks on your door, always with an urgent problem … how can you even begin to take control? This is the problem of 'breaking out' that has to be solved if you are to make changes in the way you cope with the flow of events and of demands continually placed upon you.

Academic life is not simply about getting more research money, writing more papers, or improving research ratings. Those who aim to become 'Masters of Time' must learn to handle outside factors with ease and yet still find time to order their lives, dealing effectively with conflicts of interest and loyalty. You will obviously want your life to contain elements such as creativity, collaboration, and social service, and these will need to be balanced against each other and juggled from minute to minute and from week to week.

The nature of the problem

After reading Chapter 2 you may have come to the conclusion that we are in a state of total disorder because of the variety of changes and pressures to which we are being subjected.

The gulf which we have to bridge is between the global and external factors and the way in which you as an individual cope with the particular hand dealt to you. In order to span that gulf we need first to have as much understanding as possible of the process we are entangled in, and we need to follow some very well-worn advice: 'Know thyself'.

In meeting demands made upon us it is necessary for us to understand both their own nature and the resources we have in ourselves to cope with them.

Becoming a 'Master of Time'

If you wish to become a 'Master of Time', you need to keep the following four key aims firmly in view:

(1) Get clear in your mind what it is that matters to you.

   Take responsibility for your own life, progress, success, time management. No-one else is going to! Only you yourself can decide what really matters. There should be pleasure in this, a sense of satisfaction. Our culture demands that we should not take pleasure in anything even remotely related to our work, or indeed to enjoy ourselves at all. This is a piece of programming, which has been drummed into most of us from our early days, that you will need to transcend.

(2) Reduce stress, tension and anxiety.

One should attempt to reduce wear and tear on oneself as much as possible. This too flies in the face of our cultural heritage, which makes a virtue of suffering, especially in the name of 'work'. Suffering is *not* a good in itself! A single-minded pursuit of untimely death from heart failure is not laudable, it is self-defeating.

(3) Know yourself.

The development of self-knowledge involves time management techniques such as knowing your best times of working and using them to your advantage; and pandering to your personal foibles, where this is good for morale and otherwise harmless. (For example, many creative geniuses are quoted as liking pencils to write with, black ink, a particular sort of typewriter, yellow paper, and suchlike.) There is nothing wrong with this if it helps you to get down to work immediately.

(4) Realise that time management is 'self-management'.

Whatever we do we *cannot* stop the clock. Since we *can* make better use of time, we are led to the conclusion that 'time management' is really a mode of 'self-management'. To get time under our control there are no magic tricks, only a small number of techniques which help us to form good habits of time management.

Achieving a measure of self-knowledge is probably the most important initial step. Working to become a 'Master of Time' involves a three-stage learning process, which we introduce next, to sustain and improve your performance.

(1) You must want to break out of the spiral. (Motivation)

(2) You must not to be discouraged by your first efforts even if they appear feeble. (Determination)

(3) You must sustain your efforts until the desired result is attained. (Persistence)

By following the steps in this learning process, you can now achieve what you set out to achieve – thus mastery brings its own rewards. In addition you need to be able to tolerate ambiguity and uncertainty, and you must be able to keep your mind flexible. It is in these qualities that we begin to discern the characteristics of the true researcher. Thus at this point we propose that you undertake a research project on time management.

In order to explain this we need to consider those features of the research method that are most appropriate to time management.

The research method

The type of research that we recommend for developing one's own management of time is 'action research'. This is research into a mode of solving a problem, or improving conditions in some way. We conduct it by intervening actively in the real world, not by means of an experiment in a laboratory. Unlike research in pure mathematics or philosophy involving pure concepts and deeper understanding, interesting and important as they are, this is empirical research where we need facts from the world. Essentially, the research method we should adopt consists of the three basic elements as shown in Figure 3.1. This is a research project directed towards the attainment of human happiness.

In action research of this kind you need first to observe and gather the facts, then by reflecting on and evaluating the results you can plan a course of action.

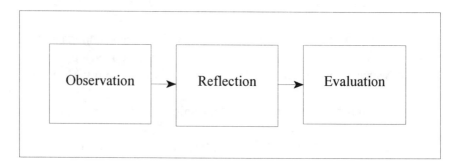

Figure 3.1: The basic research method

These three elements can thus be expanded into a nine-step plan which allows us both to research the topic and also to continue to refine and modify our research technique.

(1) State the problem.

(2) Observe the situation.

(3) Reflect on and evaluate the situation.

(4) Plan a course of action.

(5) Carry out the plan.

(6) Monitor to see that the plan is carried out and what the effects are.

(7) Pause for review of activity, using the chosen measures or character-izations of success/failure.

(8) Modify the plan.

(9) Repeat 5-8 as necessary

The important point here is that you make decisions for yourself about the frame and the objectives. What we offer to you is a higher-level framework within which those elements can be used to improve overall performance. We promise you that there will be long-term benefits. Having a procedure like this also offers a very significant immediate benefit, which derives from the principle that 'a problem that is being worked on is being managed'. That is to say, as soon as you feel that you are understanding and engaging with the problem, then the personal threat which it presents is already much reduced.

In this chapter we shall examine only stages one and two of the research method outlined above. This will enable us to state the problem and begin to observe, gathering data on the three main aspects of our problem – teaching, research and administration. Other stages in the method will be taken up in Chapter 7 and developed further.

State the problem

You will be starting with a problem that presents itself as a 'time' problem: you do not have enough time to meet some demands placed upon you, or to achieve an objective you have set yourself. Alternatively, you may identify as the main problem a lack of control over use of time because plans you make are being overturned by interruptions, by events that call for urgent and immediate action ('fire-fighting'), or by impositions of new deadlines by authorities in a position to make demands upon you. Such problems often appear intractable *as they present themselves*. What is needed in such cases is to gain a perspective on the problem that suggests how it might be made more tractable.

We shall now present four frameworks to help you to gain such a perspective. We call these

(1) The demand-supply model

(2) The ACE model

(3) The incremental or iterative model

(4) The NSS model

Choose whichever appeals to you as fitting your leading time management problem, and use it as a way to assist you in observing and analysing your situation.

To illustrate how the problem-description model might be applied, we offer examples in each case by applying the model both to a teaching example and to an administrative example. There is nothing privileged about the way in which we have applied the models; you are free to interpret these cases differently.

The demand-supply model

In order to apply this model, you will need to be able to describe your problem by using the metaphor of a *flow* of tasks through your personal work-space.

'Demands' flow in, we 'supply' time and effort, achievements (completed projects) flow out. So the current tasks (the 'whats' of the problem) are only particular instances that are stuck somewhere between initial demand and the achievement of final output.

Thus we describe our problem as one where the inflow of 'demands' is too great for our processing powers, so that the conversion part of the system is clogged (there are stacks of 'pending' paper and tasks). This particular model is crude, but it offers a first disentanglement of threads: the role of the inflow of demands is disentangled from that of the processing capacity of the person's own work-system.

It invites two independent strategies for recovery: cut the inflow, or increase the capacity. (There are two ways of increasing capacity: (1) by working faster, (2) by finessing some tasks by dropping standards.)

Example A: keeping up with a course you are teaching.

> The *demand* you are required to meet is to meet the class in two-hour-long periods each week, and to conduct the classes (whether by lecturing or other means) to satisfy governing criteria. The *supply* on your side is of preparation and contact time, and background knowledge, prepared materials etc.

Example B: dealing with applications for admission.

> This type of administrative task lends itself readily to a *flow analysis*: application forms flow in from a 'source', are dealt with, and then dispatched to a 'sink'. (One way of describing flows is as a movement between a 'source' and a 'sink'. The terminology is due to Rock-Evans, 1989.)

The ACE model

In this way of thinking about the problem we try to separate the contributions of three components 'A', 'C, and 'E' which are:

'Agent':

> the subject or client, with knowledge, skills, and ways of working;

'Challenge':

> that is, the 'demand' of the previous model;

'Environment':

> from which the challenge comes, to which results are delivered, and which remains present throughout as a shifting backdrop to our activity. In the environment will be all the elements outside the agent's immediate control or authority, but where new forms of support might be found – a new computer, better filing tools, even more clerical help.

If the 'agent' is not coping, this should be recognizable as their failure to deliver an adequate response to the 'challenge'. To match 'challenge' and 'agent' better, this schema suggests that one or the other needs to change. An 'agent' might change by learning new skills, or by developing new systems for coping with the workflow. A 'challenge' (or total set of 'challenges') might be changed by cutting down the demands. The 'environment' is the source of challenges, and the recipient of completed work. Whereas at the moment of a single snapshot the 'environment' is fixed, it may be possible to arrange for it to be made more supportive, or perhaps less demanding.

Example A: keeping up with a course you are teaching.

> You are the *agent*, applying your subject-knowledge, skills in lecturing and conducting classes, and whatever system you adopt to prepare for classes, manage the paperwork involved, structure lectures, etc. The *challenge* (as noted) is the *demand* of the previous model: to meet the class in two-hour-long periods each week, and to conduct the classes satisfactorily. This model allows us to give a place to the source of the *demand* in the *environment*, which is complex, as it involves both the enrolment of the students (when they first cross the outer 'boundary' of the course) and the various requirements placed on a teacher of the present course (by regula-tions, by the published syllabus, and so on). The *environment* also includes the various audiences there are for the course – potentially a departmental assessor, external assessors, and any 'consumers' of

graduates who may be looking for particular knowledge and skills on the part of the students after the course has ended.

Example B: dealing with applications for admission.

You as the *agent* bring knowledge of your department's admissions targets (number, and school examination performance), skills used in assessing applications, and your or the department's system for dealing with applications. The *challenge* is to meet the targets. The *environment* produces the applications, and receives your decisions; it may also provide clerical support for your work. The procedures which you need to follow to register your decisions are governed by rules and regulations, in this case set up at national level.

The incremental or iterative model

There is an iterative element in the research method mentioned above. We develop one strand of that further in this section.

The basic idea is that, 'if at first you don't succeed, try, and try, and try again!'. The value of trying *again* (iteration) derives from the incremental (or 'monotonic') features of the process: at each iteration, something needs to be done to make more success likely at the next iteration. It is not *mere* repetition: what is repeated is a 'test-operate-test' sequence where the operation is reviewed and adjusted at each test after the first.

The other special feature of this model is that it does not rely on any particular inspiration or insight in order to get started. It involves a self-conscious application of a basic principle of spontaneous human learning: 'try anything once', note the effects, then try something a bit different ... Usually we can think of *something* to try that might just help with our problem, but we are not sure whether it will do the trick. If we apply the incremental model, we do not hesitate to act, but we do make sure that we note the effects of our action, so that we can modify what we do next time. Evidently it helps to have a test-rig; some way of measuring the degree of success. In many time-sensitive activities, the time taken offers a simple criterion that we can readily apply.

We do not suggest that you use a too-rigid quantitative system of measurement. You do need, however, some idea of what counts as success, and (more important) what counts as improvement. Counting discrete items (such as to-do items) or measuring continuous quantities (time, as estimates and as time actually taken) is easy for most of us. Estimating how long it will take to complete some new project is hard if not impossible. It is here that time-diaries come into their own.

What the incremental model adds to the previous models is the element of 'negative feedback'. Not only are standards applied, they are brought to bear on your practice at the next iteration. What we notice in the examples we have chosen is that the feedback cycles can be very long, in university work; but that we can also usually find shorter ones that are more useful for tuning activity from day to day. (A point for all of us who mark or grade students' work in 'formative' assessments: the promptness of feedback is known to be a significant variable in determining its effect. Delayed feedback has little influence on behaviour.)

Example A: keeping up with a course you are teaching.

A suitable test-rig might involve taking all your work for a class in a single week, recording it, and then reviewing it at the end of the week, in the hope of finding some ways of improving your perform-ance, especially in relation to the time taken. By using the week as the unit of assessment, you provide a framework for repetitions that occur ten or more times, once for each week in the teaching term. Arguably the most apt unit of observation for a complete course is a full term, or a full year. Negative *feedback* comes from the students' course-assessments and from their examination performances. Such annual cycles provide one relevant frame for many academic activities; for us as for other learners, the long lead-times and slow feedback cycles make it difficult to apply them effectively.

Example B: dealing with applications for admission.

A minimum unit for evaluation might be provided by your work on a single application form. This is clearly a repeating element in this task. We apply iterative models to tasks of this kind almost without thinking. It is easy for us precisely because the units are readily identifiable, and the time one unit takes is short (within 15 minutes, perhaps). The problem in this case is to find a test-rig that can be used without waiting nine months for the student to appear in his first tutorial, or three years and nine months for the student to graduate.

When we are *learning* a job like this by making judgments alongside a more experienced person, we can hope for rapid feedback. This is how most of us learned to mark examination scripts, by making provisional judgments and checking them against those of more experienced markers. As with any repeatable activity, we are easily able to record the time it takes to complete the task. But not any way of speeding up the process will be acceptable, and the correctness or appropriateness of the judgment is hard to determine. ('Time and motion study', which has long since been discredited even in working environments where simple and repetitive manufacturing tasks are performed, cannot be applied at all if there is no convenient test of adequacy for task completion.)

The NSS model

This model is a robust one with applications to many time management problems. It perhaps fits best those situations where we can identify and list tasks and find that they are (apparently) too numerous to be coped with. It then invites us to identify two likely key aspects of the problem: the standards we are seeking to meet, and the speed at which we complete particular (more or less routine) tasks. 'N', 'S' and 'S' are the

> **N**umber of projects, to-do items – the challenge or demand (by item count).

> **S**tandards set for adequate completion of project/item – the quality aspect of the demands, taken severally – how well you feel it has to be done, what standards are set by the other in the contract.

> **S**peed of dealing with project/item – skill, good systems etc. The 'agent' aspect which determines how well the 'supply' of time and effort is used to achieve what, after all, you decide to achieve.

Example A: keeping up with a course you are teaching.

> The *standards* are easy to identify in this case. *Speed* likewise can be measured. It is not clear in our example of an individual course what we can count. Evidently in teaching practice, there are countable elements, for example, the number of different courses or modules

we have to teach in any given year, and the number of students enrolled in each of our courses. These measures are commonly used in loading systems for teaching. When you consider ways of reducing the total time and effort-costs of teaching a fixed or even increasing number of students, an application of the NSS model can help to bring the focus on to (an average) cost per student.

Example B: dealing with applications for admission.

The NSS model fits this case well. We can count the number of applications we have to deal with. We can note how long dealing with a single application takes. (This time will vary, depending on the complexity of the case, whether we need to invite for interview, etc.) But as with the incremental model, we find some difficulty in determining the relevant standard to apply. This is not a defect of the model, but rather a feature of the example. Compare the anecdote about the tutor who used the 'staircase' marking system: throw the scripts downstairs, and give first class marks to those that land on the top stair, upper second class marks to those that land on the next stair, and so on. This is a very time-efficient way of working, but is unlikely to meet governing quality criteria. In the marking case, we can readily supply alternative criteria. In the case of admissions work, the criteria lie ahead, in the long-term effects of decisions. In all such cases with 'feedback loops' that take a long time, we do well to draw on past experience and research, to inform value-judgments about current practice.

Choose the framework or elements of these frameworks that personally appeal to you and use them as a perspective to view the next stages of our research method.

Observe the situation

Now that you have selected a framework you can begin to observe the problem by preparing a list of all the things that you are involved in over the next week. Depending on the termly/yearly cycle of your work you will need to do this at frequent intervals, but to start with it is best to prepare only the week ahead.

Classify these activities under headings like:

Teaching

Research

Administration

In Chapters 4 to 6 you will see that we have suggested some of the topics that fall under these three main headings. You may like to look quickly at them to pick out helpful sub-headings that match your own activities.

Having listed the likely areas of work you expect to cover, you will find it useful to keep a time-diary for one full week, to obtain firm information about what is happening to your time in particular. For most purposes, an entry at 15-minute intervals will suffice; but longer periods of work on a single task will not need repeated entries. Whether you keep this diary on sheets of paper, on the pages of a large desk-diary, or on a computer file, is a matter of your own convenience. If you have not performed this exercise before, you should find the results illuminating. Repeating it occasionally will help to develop your sense of time, as well as providing much valuable information to use in planning future activity.

This is not just a one-off task, for the rhythms and academic tasks vary through the year and it will be necessary to repeat the exercise frequently.

In the following three chapters we consider teaching, research and administration in more detail. We pick up the research plan again in Chapter 7, and suggest how one might reflect upon and evaluate the information gained so far.

➡ ⬅

Summary of Chapter 3

In this chapter a nine-step research plan is presented as a way of breaking out of the time management problems you may be having. Four frameworks for the first step 'stating the problem' were considered. Main activities to be observed in the second step are teaching, research and administration. The concept of becoming a 'Master of Time' was introduced.

➡ ⬅

4 Teaching

This chapter considers the various activities involved in teaching. When you have determined which of them are chiefly responsible for absorbing your own time, you can reflect on and evaluate your own situation. Suggestions for reducing the time-costs of teaching are offered.

When you have read and acted on this chapter you will:

(1) have observed, listed and timed your teaching activities;

(2) have reflected on the difference between teaching and learning;

(3) have considered course design as a four stage process;

(4) have reviewed seven ways of containing the time-costs of teaching a typical course.

We have seen how 'the world we struggle in' is in constant change. The university system is now a mass system. The characteristics of students have changed. There are more international students, and more mature students. All these changes have consequences for teaching methods.

Another factor which affects our workload, and the effectiveness of our teaching, is the preparedness of our new students when they start at the university. Many colleagues report increasing problems in teaching first year courses. Widening access and increased recruiting of international students with different educational backgrounds will only add to such problems. The normal response would be to teach the students more, not less.

Accountability – the situation worsens

Teaching workload, as a quantifiable aspect of the teaching role, is driven by student numbers, locally agreed arrangements of course structure, choice etc; by collegial pressures influencing teaching methods and practice; and (latterly) by the perceived requirements of external quality audit and assessment.

The university teacher, like other professionals in British public sector employment, is increasingly subject to forms of external scrutiny and control in the conduct of his or her teaching tasks. Ten years ago very few British university teachers had suffered the indignity of having a colleague audit one of their lectures, let alone sit in on one of their tutorials. The teaching activity, so 'public' to the students, was private as between colleagues. But no longer: probation and progression rules have come to require such auditing, and the quality assessment system has introduced external auditing.

There have been externally-driven developments such as the growth of student questionnaires, and the introduction or strengthening of personal ('moral') tutoring systems.

Teaching/learning methods

In public discussion of university teaching it has become fashionable to speak of 'teaching and learning' and to place a new emphasis on student learning as distinct from teachers' activity. Our concern here is with the use of teachers' time. We need to be clear on terminology, and on its distinctions.

What takes teachers' time is what *they* do. The learning we are interested in goes on in the student, and results from activities that take up the *students'* time. Some of the student activity takes place in the company of teachers: 'contact time' in lectures, seminars, classes or in the laboratory. Other student activity takes place without using teacher time: 'private study'. If we were concerned with the total university time-economy, we might further analyse students' use of private-study time to separate those activities, such as work in the library or on university computers, that depend on other university staff spending time in support; and those activities that require no university staff time at all, such as reading at home.

Not all that 'teachers' do is *teaching* in the traditional sense: lecturing, conducting classes on a school model, close tutorial supervision. Chairing a small-group discussion is not teaching in this traditional sense, if all the 'teacher' does is to mediate a discussion based on a student's presentation. In some faculties, a new term, 'course-manager' (or 'module-manager') has come into use to collect the totality of tasks that a teacher performs to make a course happen, including preparing written material for distribution, placing materials on computer servers for students to access, setting and marking written work, and examining – as well as the more traditional forms of teaching.

Thus behind the phrase 'teaching and learning' we can discern activities of both teacher and learner. The teachers do far more than 'teach' in the narrow sense. The learners' time-consuming activities are a separate matter, and of only indirect interest to us here. But we note that there is a distinction between learning *activity*, and learning as the *result* of the activity. Attending lectures, reading, writing essays, performing experiments, take up time. It is not guaranteed how much learning results from spending time in this way. Like teaching staff, students have their own 'productivity' problem. The teachers' productivity problem, which we return to below, is to bring about *student learning* in the minimum of teachers' time. What we do with our time is to cause students to spend some part of their time in learning activities. What counts is how productive for the student's learning those particular activities are.

Our own focus will necessarily be on teacher activity, but will not be restricted to 'teaching' in the narrow traditional sense. We shall often speak of 'teaching' but as a shorthand for all 'course-management' activity. There are both conventional lecturing and the more 'student-centred' methods of teaching to take into consideration, such as the following:

- Lecture or conventional class teaching

  We should ask whether the product of teacher style, and skill with class size and mood, is such that individual students feel that they are participants rather than mere observers. Does the typical (not excessively shy) student feel able to raise a hand to ask a question?

- Small group teaching

  This is distinguished by the process rather than simply by number. There are many ways of managing these events. For example, a rota of students' papers or presentations puts each student in turn not only into the room but in the spotlight; how does the teacher respond (right down to keeping total silence while students debate)? Are students both recognized and rewarded for their efforts; or are they humiliated?

- Laboratory work

  This is concerned with the individual, although we should remember that help with practical work is generally provided by teachers and demonstrators.

Trying to treat the students as individuals, if not in lectures then in seminars or tutorial groups, adds to the strain of teaching larger numbers, in larger classes, with larger piles of marking. Marking is much as it always was, except that the pile is larger. Many modules – including those for first year classes of hundreds of students – involve 'tutorial' groups of not more than, say, fifteen students, that is, groups where the tutor/teacher will come to know every student's name.

It would be helpful to distinguish between 'teacher-centred' and 'student-centred' methods.

'Student-centred' methods

We need to recognize

(1) the degree to which the *student* feels his or her individuality is recognized and accepted;

(2) the extent to which the *teacher* knows and accepts each individual student.

More 'student-centred' methods can give students space to be individual, without calling on the teacher to give individual tutorials to each one of a class of a hundred and fifty.

'Teacher-centred' methods

Here the teacher is the centre of activity and control. As class size rises, whole-class teaching becomes vulnerable to de-personalization of students.

The two key elements in students' individuality should be

(1) that students are known as individuals and by name by their teachers (and by the departmental secretaries and other support staff);

(2) that in their responses to student contributions – questions, written assignments, tutorials etc. – the teachers show a sensitivity to the material which has been presented by the individual.

Staff effort is not the only input into the learning process. There are library and laboratory provisions, the residence facilities (for those using university accommodation), the ambience of the department; and then there are the other supports, such as computer provision; and field courses and other such activities in particular subjects.

If we then consider the total input to the learning process we find a difficult equation with many variables. What are the essential factors which promote and encourage student learning? Is it 'learning resources' such as laboratories, libraries and computer clusters, or is it the presence of a teacher as academic mentor? If (as we suspect) all of these are required, is there a right balance among them? How should time and money be distributed between the different forms of support for learning? There is no easy answer at the present time. There are relevant differences between disciplines, related intimately to their content. The humanities and much of the social sciences are interpretative; the teacher is also an interpreter. Humanists cannot see how students can be helped, unless it is with the support of a teacher as interpreter. It is their standard practice always to disagree (in detail) with other books and articles they introduce to their students, and to feel a responsibility for showing the students what is wrong with them. Not to offer criticisms would be an abdication of their responsibility for the students' learning.

In such subjects, teaching involves inculcating critical skills. We must bear in mind that we may not be as confident in teaching critical skills, which are not articulated, only practised, as we feel in teaching our own criticisms (and hoping the skills rub off). Teaching critical skills is more costly in time than teaching our own views. Carefully structured critical readings and discussions of texts are needed. It is not easy to trust students to teach themselves critical reading without considerable support from teachers.

In science things appear to be much more cut and dried, and the emphasis for the teacher is usually in delivering a body of knowledge, and in helping the student to acquire a range of practical skills.

Teaching and learning

A first attempt at defining the time management problem for teaching might take the following form:

> it is to maximize all student learning, between the first-year registration and graduation, for minimum cost in staff time.

It is unfortunate that this definition is somewhat senseless as it stands. It can be compared with an imaginary aim of motor car design:

> it is to ensure that the car travels at maximum speed using the minimum of petrol.

How do you compare 'car A' which can cruise at 30 mph and expends one gallon of fuel in 100 miles, with 'car B' that cruises at 60 mph but expends three gallons of fuel in 100 miles? Should we maximize student learning per hour of staff effort (or equivalently, minimize staff effort per unit of student learning – whatever that might be)? As we need then to bring speed into the picture in relation to the car, so in the case of learning, we require a suitable standard of achievement. In practice we use quality at graduation as our standard. So we might re-state the aim thus:

> it is to get students to a minimum standard for the BA/BSc, at minimum cost in staff time.

However, that is still not a good enough aim for our current purposes. We want each student to get the *best* BA/BSc of which he or she is capable. Certainly we should not be satisfied, nor would the assessors, with graduating classes where all students were awarded third-class degrees. Taking all this into account, perhaps the best way to state the aim is as follows:

> it is to keep graduation standards up while minimizing costs in staff time and effort;

expecting that the minimum cost in staff time will be a good deal less than we have been accustomed to paying in recent years.

The productivity problem

Adopting the standard achieved by graduating students as our test of 'teaching quality' seems right. And benchmarking this using recent results is appropriate and acceptable. The goal of time-control for teaching then becomes

> to minimize teacher time spent in enabling students to achieve this standard.

 The less time we spend, while still obtaining that result, the more productive we are as teachers.

We need a measure of productivity. A crude and simple approach might be to sum together all the teaching time devoted to one year-group of students in a degree programme, and to set that against the average degree class achieved by that group. From such statistics we could derive a value, representing staff hours per class point. To raise productivity, we would then reduce the staff hour value while keeping the average degree class constant. Clearly enough, we have no hope of applying this approach directly, as the degree class is awarded at the very end of the teaching process. If we wish therefore to practise 'evidence-based teaching' we have to obtain our evidence elsewhere.

To raise productivity – to increase student learning in relation to staff time given to teaching – we should ideally draw on research that evaluates teaching methods and supports for student learning, to ensure that our time is used most productively. Attempts have indeed been made, usually in the context of evaluating new methods, to conduct such research. Sadly we cannot produce for you the three clear results that enable us to organize all our teaching to be maximally efficient. 'Teaching methods' are hard to describe and to classify. 'Student learning' as a desired outcome, is always influenced by many other factors than the teaching method – such as library and laboratory provision, not to mention the support of other students. And we all know from our own experience that the value of some teaching activity is determined as much by the individual characteristics of the teacher as by the method. Not all lecture courses are equally valuable; but they all use the lecture method.

In the absence of helpful research results, we must appeal to other principles to help ourselves along. In our teaching activities as in other areas of our work, two approaches to method are possible:

(1) a conservative approach

(2) a radical approach

The conservative approach leaves methods in place, but seeks to reduce the time-costs of each element. An example is the reduction of the time-cost of marking by abolishing double-marking. Another familiar conservative time-saver is the reduction of the number of courses or modules, wherever this can be achieved, so that economies of scale (in contact time) result.

The radical approach involves 'process re-engineering'. To apply this approach we would need to stand back from the traditional methods and the detail, and to review what the objectives of the whole exercise are: in this case, the maintenance of standards at graduation. We would then look freshly at what activities students might need to be involved in between first registration and the very last examination in order to ensure that this object-ive was achieved. With staff-time at a premium, we should certainly place high value on forms of 'private study' wherever they can be seen as pro-ductive. Because different students have different needs, and different learning styles, it is most unlikely that we should find that a uniform system under which all students were treated in the same way, would emerge as the best choice. *Teaching* would almost certainly need to be replaced by *tutoring* to guide and support students in their use of the learning resources provided for them.

Radical as this approach may seem, in relation to the more traditional forms of university teaching, it is being actively promoted in some quarters as we write. (If you also suspect that the approach involves the re-invention of a very old-fashioned wheel, we do not deny you the right to do so.) Before we can say that it will save on staff time, it will be necessary to quantify the costs in tutorial time and to assess the large investments that would be required in such non-teaching facilities as libraries, which in most United Kingdom universities are under-resourced to support a large increase in private study activity among students.

A view of student learning that emphasized the standard at graduation, and opened up the possibility of a variety of individual paths towards that goal, would require the demolition of much of the structure of degree programmes as sets of individual courses – a structure that has been reinforced by recent developments of credit-based learning and a fragment-ation of teaching into small 'modules' each with its own examination.

So in addressing the reader working in the real world, we confidently put the radical option to one side, and focus on 'conservative' approaches to time management for teachers.

The activity of the teacher

For individual academics the time management problem is probably seen in the more concrete terms of their own activities:

> I have to design, write and deliver a number of new courses and have them ready by the beginning of next term.

In considering the time management implications of this, the process of course design can be viewed in terms of a simple teaching/learning model:

(1) Set aims and objectives of the course.

(2) Determine structure and syllabus.

(3) Select teaching/learning methods.

(4) Assess what students have learned (that is, evaluate and assess).

Aims and objectives

Here are some aims taken from a university prospectus which show the university's realization of the need for accountability to the world outside and for developing each student for his or her future career. It also shows how the pressure is on the academic to produce goods saleable in today's market.

> Education
>
> > You will develop the knowledge, skills and understanding necessary for successful teaching in primary school.

Biological sciences

> You will develop your understanding of the latest developments in animal and plant biotechnology.

Engineering

> We help to produce engineers who are prepared for the requirements of the engineering profession in Europe through the 1990s and in to the twenty-first century.

When we look at the objectives we see they get down more to the nitty gritty; for example in Education:

> on completion of this course the student will be able to:

- give the three basic components of any learning theory;

- describe the characteristics which distinguish a theory of learning from a theory of teaching.

Structure and syllabus

Designing the structure and syllabus needs first to take into account the slot within the overall degree structure into which the course will fit, then the broad subject areas that should be considered. These are first put in order then the detailed subject content for each course or module is determined.

Even in this first part of course design the teacher has to employ a whole range of skills, from keeping up with (and initiating) the latest research to organizational skills required for putting this in a structured syllabus.

If you are not practised in all these skills, and many academics at the start of their career are not, then you will have time management problems. These will arise at least in part from the fact that it takes time to 'get up to speed' when learning a new skill. With many motor skills the differences are dramatic. The facts are more elusive in the case of intellectual skills, but it is wise always to allow for the possibility that as you repeat a performance, for example a lecture course, you will find everything becomes much easier and less time-consuming. Conversely, you need to allow for the likelihood that your first outing will require extra time and effort, and you should not be discouraged by that.

Now let us turn to what teaching methods are available to us.

Teaching/learning methods

A search of the university literature aforementioned revealed the following:

lectures

tutorials

seminars

practicals

fieldwork

It is interesting to see that the prospectus used the number of students in the group as the criterion for using different methods:

tutorials – small groups of up to five for individual contact between staff and students;

seminars – groups of up to twenty allowing time for discussion and debate;

lecture – talk to hundreds.

Further investigation of the literature of the university in question enabled us to extend this list as follows:

Audio and video recordings

Case study workshops

Computer-aided exercises

Computer assisted learning

Dissertations

Excavations

Games

Group discussions

Group projects

Language classes

Music lessons

Personal study/private study

Presentations

Problem-solving classes

Project design

Project work

Role play (simulations)

Self-study workshops

Although this is a more comprehensive list, preparation and delivery time will vary tremendously with the effectiveness of the learning. In time management terms some guidelines on the advantages, disadvantages, and time implications in preparation and delivery of these methods are necessary. A useful and continuing departmental activity would be for all who engage in different teaching/learning techniques to pool their knowledge so that new staff could have the benefit of others' experience – helping their time planning. (This team activity is taken up again in Chapter 9.)

There can of course be huge variations between teachers, and for the same teacher between courses, in the amount of 'private study' time the teacher puts in around a single course, including not only reading-around and preparation of lectures and materials, but also formative assessment, time on group-work, even time spent on responding to enquiries from individual students. If the teacher gets the reputation of being 'approachable', it can cost … in his or her time! There is a conflict here. Giving more time per student takes more of our own time, but (we tend to assume) ensures that the student learns more. We do however need to watch out for that over-dependency which the *teacher* finds rewarding, not necessarily to the benefit of the student. (The teacher ministers to dependent students, blames the government for his or her excessive workload, but actually he or she is enjoying feeling wanted!)

Now you should be ready to consider what we have listed as stage 3 of the research process in Chapter 3 – 'evaluating and reflecting'. Here you should assess whether your teaching is expensive in terms of your own time and if so in what ways your methods could change without diminishing your standards.

Evaluating and reflecting

This is where you have to reflect on your own course load in relation to the lists given above. Are there any areas where you can cut down, change and/or save time? In order to help you in this we suggest some ways of containing your time-costs in the stages of conducting a typical taught course (and using common current practice – nothing revolutionary!):

- Minimize the number of courses/modules you teach (departmental).

- Negotiate a coherent teaching load so that your courses have related content. (Arrange to give courses in areas you need to research.)

- Use textbooks. Recognize that most students do not read voraciously, or pursue references with enthusiasm. Ensure they have a firm core of reading, for texts available for purchase and also stocked in multiple copies in the library. Reduce the total content of what you prepare, but make a point of providing lists of supplementary reading (there is no need to have read every word yourself – a very expensive form of perfectionism!) for the more able and inquisitive. Good textbooks in the science area can help students working in the laboratory and so reduce teacher contact time – though not the time taken in laboratory supervision.

- Minimize contact time for yourself (teacher-student time), in relation to student-student contact and discussion time: by using methods that divide a larger class into small groups ('buzz groups', 'syndicates' – any group methods where the teacher is able to leave the class at work once the process has started).

- Computer assisted learning, audio-visual methods etc. can and do help (in some if not all disciplines). We expect further developments in the near future in exploiting information technology for learning.

- Examining: do not over-assess. Use only as much examination material as you need to reach a grade for the student. Replace double-marking with monitored single-marking.

- 'Formative assessment' is of value to student learning, but can be very time-consuming. Commentary on students' work from post-graduate tutors, or from other students (in peer-assessment programmes) can be helpful to the learner and take the place of most of the work done by teachers.

Summary of Chapter 4

This chapter was designed to help you to think about your own teaching and the time it takes. We considered the difference between teaching and learning and course design in terms of a simple four factor teaching/learning model involving setting aims and objectives, determining structure and syllabus, selecting suitable teaching/learning methods, and assessing what has been learned. Seven ways of containing time-costs in the stages of teaching a typical course were offered.

5 Research

This chapter considers research: the unpredictable nature of the process of illumination, and the many complexities and day-to-day research work. It is to the latter that this chapter is mainly addressed.

When you have read and acted on this chapter you will:

(1) know the activities in research that are susceptible to time management techniques;

(2) have considered your own research activities using the research model described in Chapter 3;

(3) have looked in detail at the following aspects of research activity: reading, thinking and writing, and obtaining grants.

Why should we be concerned about managing research time at all, since

(a) not all academics are 'research-active';

(b) research (surely) is what we save time from other activities *for*, not something to be cut down itself?

The romantic idea of the 'pure researcher' who sits and meditates until the inspiration dawns, is far removed from the daily activity of researchers in most academic disciplines, even the most theoretical (such as pure mathematics or philosophy). Most research involves a good deal of 'busy work' and organization. Questions of efficiency can be raised about these activities. We should not forget, though, that amongst the constraints on time that affect all researchers, there is the unpredictable nature of the process of illumination which produces the new idea. The unconscious, from which new ideas (occasionally) emerge, does not follow strict schedules, and when it does deliver its gifts it is then that we may need to take time to reflect on them and to record them, whatever else we had planned to be doing at the time.

The rhythms of research can readily cut across the more predictable rhythms of teaching. Examples abound; here is just one: a friend of ours is an astrophysicist and optical astronomer. He needs to book time on telescopes in distant countries, as and when he can obtain the time-slots that also suit his programme of research. Although he can usually avoid the teaching terms, he is often required to spend two to three weeks abroad at periods when one or another of the telescopes in question is free, regardless of other commitments at the home university.

We shall approach our topic using the research method which we have described in Chapter 3.

Observe, reflect and evaluate

We shall delineate the main aspects of research so that you can observe your own activities and then reflect on and evaluate them:

- Academics are trained (most intensively, for longest) as practitioners of their own disciplines. They are professional … physicists, classicists, fuel engineers, anatomists. It is unlikely that someone who is not schooled to a high level in the same discipline can understand all the factors that enter into their research, indeed into their use of time. Whatever ideas an outsider can offer need to be interpreted within the discipline by practitioners.

- Research involves creative work, getting new ideas, inspiration; there are no algorithms for inspiration, with or without time-parameters. Bear in mind that in addition to the core of inspiration, research activity covers many different modes of work, from preparation to the writing-up of results, that do have connections with time. If you waste valuable time commuting to work (amid traffic too distracting to enable you to think about anything else) and we were to show you a short-cut which gets you to work in half the time, we would have helped you to find more time for your research, and without in any way encroaching on your professional territory.

■ Even with respect to the intimate core of a subject, the auto-biographies of great scientists and scholars, and some psychological research, suggest that there are some ways of working which may be more productive than others.

The difficulty of focusing on research activity derives not only from the inwardness of particular disciplines, but also from the great variety of activities in which researchers may be involved. Most researchers have to work some time at their desks, if only to write their applications for grant-aid, their reports and learned articles. In the humanities, in some areas of the social sciences, and at the 'theoretical' end of the mathematical sciences, work with books and papers, either at one's own desk or in the library, forms the main activity of research.

A new dimension enters when research in a subject involves a distinctive practical element. Laboratory and field-work involve many different styles of work in different disciplines. Working with wholly inanimate materials, as in most physics or engineering laboratories, and working with animals or with human subjects presents very different challenges and involves many different routines.

Among the possible components of desk-work already mentioned was the completion of applications for research grants. Alongside the non-practical/practical divide is another divide, among university research workers, into those whose research normally requires some such additional funding – to keep a research laboratory up to date, or to finance the provision of expensive consumable materials, or perhaps travel to distant locations – and those whose research can usually be conducted even without any such special funding.

Where research funding is forthcoming, the research involved is tightly structured around a declared research project, contributory as it may be to a larger research programme. Such projects have a beginning, a middle, and an end, with some reporting and publication requirements built into the contract. In many cases also, research funding permits or involves either the recruitment and training of research assistants, or the supervision of research students whose work is part of the project.

Where there are also laboratories to be organized and supervised, a senior researcher or team-leader will be involved, as part of his or her research activity, in supervising other people working on the project, including other academic staff, research assistants and laboratory staff. Research work of this kind, therefore, involves people-management. Thus research can manifest *many* dimensions of complexity; and problems in apportioning time can involve *any* of them.

To cut some path through the jungle of complexity and variety that research activity amounts to, we shall use a simplifying framework – drawing on the set of contrasts above (desk, library, practical work, grant-aid, team-work in research).

We think of research as being conducted in a field or area of interest, where the researcher has some professional background already, no doubt, but where also they need to keep up with current work, to be aware of published material both old and new.

Against the background of this understanding, the researcher develops one or more research programmes. A programme will be driven by a question or questions, to which they seek answers; where those answers will advance the subject. Given the programme, particular projects will be proposed. In a discipline which is library-based, and where the work is typically done by solitary individuals, the project may not be made any more explicit than as a plan to work on an article or book, or to write up a paper to present to a seminar. If, however, the project requires additional funding, or involves others in it too, some more formal process will be needed to define it, in terms that can be written down on a grant application form, or communicated to a co-worker who will set up some equipment, or conduct some fieldwork. The project will, in such a case, come to involve a formal contract which will define its goals, and indicate the process by which those goals will be achieved.

Throughout the period of work on the project, the larger task of monitoring the subject area continues, and as one project nears completion, the subject's 'problematic' will suggest another project, most likely within the area of the research programme. The resolving of one question will suggest new questions, and so the cycle continues.

Observing

In order to observe your own activities with regard to research you might consider them under the following headings:

- work at desk with own papers and books, and stand-alone word-processor (that is, reading, writing and thinking);

- work at desk with networked computer (with access to remote data-bases, e-lists etc.);

- work in the library (local university library, distant library holding source material, special book collections etc.);

- keeping up with the subject, monitoring journals, conferences, e-lists, colleagues' papers, etc; reading new books, reviewing books; using abstracting services;

- work with people: co-workers who fix things in the laboratory (technicians) or who are part of the research team; human subjects of field-work in social sciences etc;

- work with postgraduates and research assistants assigned to the project;

- relations with grant-awarding bodies: finding sources of funding; making applications; agreeing contracts, and programmes of completion; keeping to the contract through thick and thin; reporting the results;

- an individual project, or a limited area of interest, within the research programme, where that project may be defined by an agreement with a collaborating colleague, or a contract with a grant-awarding agency or publisher, or simply be defined (in a theoretical, individualistic discipline) as the plan to write up an article or book on one's own account.

Reflecting and evaluating

We have now reached the point where we should reflect on and evaluate our activities in terms of time. Each of the activities which have been mentioned above has many implications for your time management, but here we want to explore only two, perhaps the most fundamental ones, in greater detail:

(1) Working at your desk

(2) Keeping up with your subject and pursuing a research programme

Working at your desk

There are three activities which take place at your desk:

reading

writing

thinking

These are vital, but can also be time-consuming if not performed effectively.

Reading

Here is a brief summary of what we consider some of the most important time savers:

- Think what you are reading for, be prepared to skim, use indexes, tables of contents, cribs (summaries, reviews) as the total of possible material is far too large. Some note however brief (in a project diary) should be kept of what has been looked at, as an aid to memory.

- Marking items of text can be helpful for future reference, as it saves time in finding particular passages. When you own a book or possess photocopies of an article there is some merit in highlighting key phrases and sentences. (Never in library books!)

Writing

There are two main approaches to writing (Thomas, 1999):

(1) The classical method

In this method the writing process is considered to be putting words down on paper (or screen) to express meaning. Generating and ordering ideas is considered as a preliminary to this process. The classical method assumes that the writing follows logically.

(2) The generative method

Here writing is used to generate meaning. This assumes that we may be unsure of what we think or want to say until we write it down in words or sentences.

The classical method uses pre-planning and assumes that the process is simply the translation of meaning into words, whereas in the generative method thinking and writing interact. Meaning is thus generated by the writing. However, these methods are at two ends of a spectrum with a wide range of methods and techniques in between.

In science and engineering the writing is often pre-planned and then written one component at a time. In arts, writers often produce a whole first draft at one sitting.

Effective researchers may approach writing in many different ways, within the spectrum just mentioned. Listed below are some common ones (usually followed singly, occasionally in a combination):

- start at page one and write until you reach the end;

- write a first draft, then tear it up and re-write the entire document;

- write repeated drafts, each time modifying the last one, until you are completely satisfied with the result of your re-writing;

- decide on your tables, graphs and diagrams and then write the text in between;

- build a structure or outline and then fill this in;

- write down what you wish you could prove, or what you wish was true, then read the literature and/or do the experiments and revise or re-write the original version as required by the results of your further research.

The last method relates the writing process directly to the other research activities which it reflects. In practice, the other methods of writing for research will also interweave writing with your research activities.

Having found the method that suits you best, you should then practise it. With use you will not only gain more fluency, you will also be able to get straight down to writing, with no time lost through staring at a blank page or screen.

With all writing it is essential to remember to be careful and to keep back-up copies. Manuscripts can get lost in the post or at the publishers; they can be left on a train, stolen, or burnt accidentally; hard discs can crash, and so on.

As you know, reading and writing are actually forms of thinking. Good time management practice in any situation is to get your goals clear. Applied to reading and writing this becomes – *get your questions clear*. Stop and think before you start reading or writing; ask yourself what you are trying to achieve, and try to keep the 'main question' in mind as you read, or write.

Treat reading and writing like a conversation; thus, reading is the author in conversation with you, and you are permitted ask him questions. So as in well-ordered debate, you need to know what the *main question* is currently.

There is another point on reading which is most relevant to time-wasting: by getting your own questions clear, you can avoid being seduced into the author's project which is typically different from your own.

In writing you are leading the conversation but need to anticipate, as far as possible, what questions your reader will ask.

Thinking

Imagine you have a problem and do not know which way to turn. What should you do? Write down the problem as clearly as you can. Then ask yourself

> what it is that you do not understand; then,

> what it is that you cannot solve.

The effort of giving it clear verbal form, if indeed you can manage it, can sometimes help; and amounts to a marker of where you have come to.

Remember, real work is bound to have its painful side. When you are working to your utmost you are working at the limits of your comprehension.

Perhaps you are the sort of person who needs various time management techniques to free up time for real thinking; but remember there are some people who think best on their feet. There are times, after you have thought about a problem and immersed yourself in the facts, when the solution comes to you in a flash just as you are engaged in other work or relaxation.

Keeping up with your subject and pursuing a research programme

What counts as keeping up with the subject (maintaining background knowledge), having a research programme (or programmes), and having an individual project will vary between disciplines and between individuals and sub-areas of a discipline. Compare and contrast the following: keeping up with … current work on the language of the *Iliad*; current work in molecular biology; current work on unsolved problems in some area of mathematics.

In all disciplines, maintaining this background to research is likely to involve work that is biased in the direction of the desk, the networked computer, the library and talking with colleagues – even in the most practical, grant-funded and team-working disciplines.

To be pursuing (actively) a research programme is to have identified a string of issues, questions, experimental protocols, within your discipline and usually within an identified narrow area of the discipline. Effectiveness in research requires some narrower focus – as supervisors are forever trying to get across to PhD students who want to solve the 'riddle of the universe'.

It is in this aspect that conventional time management techniques help the most. (Chapter 11 contains some more suggestions of this kind.) Other aspects have been dealt with in other chapters of this book; for example, see Chapter 8 for help with paperwork of various kinds.

Teamwork in research is a particularly important topic. Here we have: delegation; interpersonal skills (assertiveness, dealing with difficult people, counselling …); planning, monitoring progress, reporting, etc. For more discussion on this see Chapter 9.

Grants and funding

The bidding systems in operation now make for a great deal of abortive work. Many researchers in the science and engineering area have no choice but to go for grants, to stay afloat at all. (And the system is moving rapidly to one where only a small sub-set of universities will be able to host research in laboratory-based sciences.) In applying for any kind of funding there is a whole sequence of events that present a challenge of time management:

- identifying needs for funding;

- identifying project to be funded;

- finding funders;

- getting and completing forms, with all that may entail by way of data on track record, refereeing etc;

- hitting deadlines; failing and beginning again; succeeding and accepting the contract; planning to fulfil the contract, including deadlines, reporting requirements;

- hiring staff; managing the team; organising/overseeing the practical work; writing-up; reporting … and then doing it all over again.

But what can usefully be said about this? It all takes a lot of valuable time, but that you know if you have ever tried. The question is, how can that time be cut down, best used? Here are some tips that may help:

(1) Spend time on investigating what organisations might give funding for your research – library research with reference books and databases.

(2) Save time by choosing a limited number of potential funders – do not scatter your research proposals over too wide an area at first.

(3) Find out all you can about your chosen funders – get their literature and talk to them over the phone, write to them and, if invited, go and see them.

(4) Write clear research proposals – go to staff development workshops on how to write grant applications.

(5) Do not begrudge the time spent when you fail. Think of it as a learning experience and try again – remember researchers are

persistent, even in the face of repeated failure. Apply your researcher principles to your grant getting.

Summary of Chapter 5

Creative work is not susceptible to strict time limits, but many aspects of research are. This chapter has described these aspects and has shown how time management techniques can be applied to them. It has considered these in terms of background work such as keeping up with the subject, and activities like working at your own desk or in the library. Methods of writing papers have been considered, and the processes involved in getting grants – two essential aspects of research work.

6 Administration

This chapter considers administration: what it is, what it is for, and how we can meet the challenge of containing its voracious appetite for time – time that we would rather spend on research or teaching.

When you have read and acted on this chapter you will:

(1) be able to analyse administrative tasks into their component activities;

(2) know how to decide whether some administrative role is worthwhile and is being performed effectively;

(3) know how to cut down on your administrative time.

Understanding administration

What do we mean by 'administration'? In the university context, the term is used loosely for anything we are required to do that is neither teaching nor research. It covers at least four different types of activity:

(1) certain tasks required as routine elements within teaching or research activity;

(2) named tasks or roles undertaken by academic staff outside their main teaching and research duties;

(3) other routine or occasional tasks such as attending departmental meetings, or fulfilling personnel roles;

(4) anything which professional administrators do.

Tasks arising

In the first group we have listed – tasks arising within teaching or research – we would count record-keeping (attendance and mark records), pursuing absentee students, applying for research grants, writing 'business plans' for research proposals, and organizing conferences and colloquia.

Named tasks

The second group is familiar: administration as the performance of one or another named administrative role. Titles will of course vary with university and department; here is a list from one department:

combined studies tutor

computing officer

convener (chair) of departmental meeting

departmental database manager

director of undergraduate studies

examinations officer

finance officer

fire & safety officer(s)

first-year tutor

head of department

information officer

tutor to junior year abroad students

library representative

MA organiser

officer for students with disabilities

part-time degree liaison officer

postgraduate admissions tutor

postgraduate research tutor

teaching quality officer

research officer

schools liaison officer

secretary to departmental meeting

senior tutor

staff development officer

staff research seminar organiser

student welfare liaison officer

telephone/reprographics officer

timetable officer

undergraduate admissions tutor

Each of the above is performed by one individual (but in some other departments are shared between several). A few tasks exist that are undertaken by many or most of the academic members of the department:

course team leader

mentor (for probationary staff)

probation supervisor

staff reviewer

The named administrative tasks range from some which take up substantial proportions of the total workload of an individual academic member of staff – up to 50 per cent of time – to others which involve only a few hours' work in a year.

Occasional tasks

The shorter list of administrative tasks above fits between the named tasks and those additional duties that fall on all members of the department or unit, for example, attending departmental meetings, or turning out for admissions open days. Usually too we do not account membership of, and attendance at, committees as a named role, but this is another form of administrative duty. These tasks make up our third group.

Administration

Our fourth category, administration, deserves a mention even in a book directed to academic staff, because it is worth clearing up possible confusions here. There is an overlap between the actual or potential duties of academic staff and of administrative staff. In the United Kingdom we have seen a steady professionalization of the administrative role during the past fifty years, against a historical background where, in the Camford College, all the administration was done by academic members (Fellows of the College). Nowadays there are jobs performed by administrators – the specialist jobs that require professional qualifications in accounting, or in law. Other generalist jobs have become so demanding and in their own way so specializ- ed that there is now no question of an academic performing them in only a part of their time while they also undertake teaching and research.

Contrariwise, there are some administrative tasks that only an academic can perform, or is allowed to perform. In most universities office-holders such as heads of departments, or deans of faculty, are academic staff who retain their stake in academic careers of research and teaching, but hold office only for a short periods (two to five years). They are entrusted with decision-making on those academic matters involving judgments of quality, which are jealously guarded within the academic profession (not only those decisions made on the quality of student work but also decisions made regarding promotions and appointments to academic posts).

For present purposes, the main moral to draw from this complexity is that we should not think of 'administration' as 'what administrators do'. Things are not so simple.

Time management problems in administration

What problems of time management does administration present? For most of us, the answer is blindingly obvious: there is far too much administration and it takes far too much time! The demands of administration appear to grow and grow without limit, and we can find several explanations for this trend:

- external demands arising from legislation – for example, safety legislation requiring that fire officers be named in workplaces; or health and safety legislation governing science laboratories;

- the growth of the 'quality industry' which records and evaluates teaching and research activity – involving audits and reports, which demand record-keeping, monitoring of activity, and periodic major assessments;

- increased competition for scarce research grant funding which drives up the level of activity in preparing applications and bids;

- a succession of national development projects where funds are distributed to universities after a competitive bidding process – from 'new blood' appointments to Teaching and Learning Technology Programme grants;

- reduced total funding per student, resulting in higher student-staff ratios, and so higher loads of administrative work related to students;

- increasing competition for 'new' types of student – international students, mature students, work-based students – with much greater demands (per student) for recruitment activity;

- extra fund-raising activity in search of additional moneys to compensate for progressive reductions in 'core' government funding;

- successive and multiple re-organizations – of teaching structures (modularisation), academic year structures (semesterisation), departmental and faculty organizational divisions, that require planning, implementation and long 'running-in' periods – to the point where continual change, involving continuous administration of change, becomes the norm.

The effects on teaching and research activity of the sheer volume of administrative work are compounded by the timing of administrative demands. Teaching and examining usually work to an annual cycle; research work has to be fitted in around that timetable, for most of us who have teaching as well as research duties. Even then, some research demands cut across the teaching, when proofs have to be read urgently, or an experiment or field investigation places 'real-time' demands upon us. The variety of unavoidable administrative tasks includes many that have their own urgent and short deadlines, which come at times that are unpredictable and often highly inopportune. Because external bodies also work to ever-shorter timescales themselves, they impose sudden and tight deadlines on those who would bid for funds, or for reporting. There are also administrative jobs that are by their nature unpredictable in their demands, as where a 'fire-service' is provided (by the departmental computer officer, for example).

The large and jagged time-demands of administrative work are unwelcome because they interfere with teaching and research. Academic staff are professionals in their subjects; they have chosen them and they usually enjoy them. Administrative work involves activities in which, as subject practitioners, they have had no previous training. The 'amateur' tradition in academic administration proposes that administration is an undemanding, but also undeserving, activity – an irritating necessity whose requirements are to be minimized. In the large modern university, and in the increasingly competitive environment in which we are placed, administration has become not only more time-consuming, but also a good deal more difficult than it used to be. So to add insult to injury, we find that we are 'de-skilled' – required to undertake activity that, sometimes, we feel none too competent at, and learning how to do such things properly only adds to our administrative loads and takes more time from teaching or research.

Solutions

There are just three ways of reducing the time-demands of administration:

   (1) reducing the time taken by individual administrative tasks;

   (2) cutting out whole tasks;

   (3) harmonizing the demands of all your projects and roles.

We shall consider these options in turn. In order to contain the costs of administration, we need an understanding of the activities that go to make up administrative work; we need to question the very point of each task and role.

Activities

As we go about performing one or another administrative task, what is it that actually takes up the time? Consideration of the detail of the job will reveal that the work involves spending time on a number of distinct activities, for example:

- receiving, holding, and storing documents;

- responding to direct approaches (in person or on the telephone);

- arranging, attending or conducting meetings or interviews;

- reading forms, reports, memoranda, or committee papers;

- obtaining information;

- imposing a structure on information, and performing queries or calculations with it;

- checking data, evaluating, assessing or scoring performances or records;

- making decisions (whether by yourself or in concert with others);

- writing memoranda, letters, reports, minutes.

For example, a departmental admissions tutor will receive and hold application forms; will read them and evaluate the application; may seek additional information, for example by contacting the candidate directly; will make a decision whether to accept or reject; and will record that decision (in a departmental record) before writing to the candidate.

Once such time-consuming activities are identified, other questions can be asked about them. Many of them can be understood as involving most or all of the following elements:

- knowledge of relevant subject-matter;

- skills exercised in the activity;

- some tools or technology;

- a system or method of performing the activity (in which the knowledge and skills are employed using the technology);

- quality aspects – the activity can be performed well or badly, with good or bad results.

In some of the activities, the elements above are so familiar as to be taken for granted. All reading requires knowledge of the language, and reading is a basic skill. The technology of reading is partly in ourselves – our eyes and hands – and partly in the documents that we read. (Structured application forms are a technical device both to organize information and to assist the reader in assimilating it.) We may read quickly or slowly, we may absorb and digest the information or fail to take it in; and the quality of this reading affects in turn the quality of the decisions we make using the information we have assimilated.

The personal and organizational aspects of paper-management are more explicit and conscious for us than are those of reading. We have therefore devoted a separate chapter to this topic (Chapter 8).

Increasingly the technology used in these activities is housed in computers – we use them to write, and we record structured information in spreadsheets and in database tables with the result that calculations and complex queries can be performed more quickly and conveniently.

Conversion processes

As we have just seen, an administrative task can be divided into separate activities. These activities can be performed well or badly, quickly or slowly. Before we can move to time-saving, we need a perspective from which we can evaluate overall effectiveness. Each administrative task has, or should have, a point; a worthwhile goal it achieves. In many cases it is helpful to think of the achievement of the goal as involving a 'conversion process' – by analogy with a production process which converts raw materials into a product. This idea has been generalized to cover much more abstract kinds of 'production', for example, the production of a new student enrolment from the 'raw material' of a completed application form, by way of a decision to accept the application. The model can even be applied, admittedly with some strain, to administrative roles that involve a 'service' element, where demands come in at random. (For example, an enquiry service might be represented as converting a puzzled customer into a satisfied, better-informed one.)

The value of this 'process' perspective for time management is that it views the task not in terms of the particular activities that have traditionally made it up, but rather in terms of the product of the task as a whole, given the starting-conditions. Particular activities are then open to critical evaluation for their contribution to the whole process. For example, a department might traditionally have interviewed all applicants for admission individually; but statistical research might reveal that the rate of interviewing appeared to have no effect on the proportion of candidates who accepted offers of places or who arrived to register the following year. Cutting the interview activity out of the process might then save time but with no loss of effectiveness in the total process. If the task had been *defined* in terms of its component activities, the possibility of such an economy of effort would have been missed.

The example just given is quite commonplace, and many academic departments will have evaluated this particular activity – interviewing candidates for admission as students – with some care. That such thinking is not always taken for granted is testified by the unfamiliarity of the concept of 'evidence-based medicine' among doctors. If we are to achieve maximum economy of administrative time, we need 'evidence-based administration' and so we also need some concepts analogous to that of recovery from an illness in the practice of medicine. We need to know how the output of our conversion process is to be evaluated.

The quality issue

Whereas we are familiar with the application of quality questions in teaching and in research, we are less familiar with them when we think about administration. Is tidiness a virtue, or can we be just as effective with a cluttered desk?

If we consider the list of activities, there seem to be far too many questions of quality that might arise. Writing that we do in the course of some administrative task may produce clumsy or elegant prose, it may be a painful or a pleasurable process, it may be easy for the audience to follow, or obscure. And so on.

We need to distinguish between standards that are

- relevant and irrelevant;

- internal and external;

- appropriate and inappropriate.

Standards that are *relevant* to the activity involve virtues that promote the quality of the ultimate product, or the effectiveness of the whole process. A symmetrical and satisfying arrangement of trays and other desk furniture may please the eye of the worker and the visitor, but is unlikely in itself to contribute to the quality of the ultimate output. On the other hand, an ergonomically effective arrangement of the workspace, with frequently-needed items close at hand, ample clear working space directly in front of the chair, and other reference material stored further away, will assist in speed of working and in effectiveness, even if the general appearance to an on-looker is not particularly pleasing.

The contrast between internal and external quality is related to the contrast between *process* and *product*. We say that quality is *internal* if it relates to some activity the value of which is only internal to the total process – it has at best an indirect effect on the product. A well-organized filing system may help the worker to work quickly and to find needed information so that decisions are better-informed. But its relation to the total output is indirect. *External* quality is the quality of the product itself: it is the quality of the result, not of the process. If we are to minimize the costs of administration, we may need ruthlessly to pursue external quality and to ensure that we do not waste time on internal quality that is strictly irrelevant to the outcome.

We want a *good* outcome; but even here, and context by context, we may need to be cautious. Not any standard that we can apply to the outcome is *appropriate*. This evaluation may be both difficult and controversial. In United Kingdom universities , one 'output' is having considerable influence, namely, the grading achieved in the Research Assessment Exercise (RAE). But the outcome of the RAE involves both a numerical grade (scale 1-5/5*) and a financial outcome. The latter depends also on the so-called 'volume measure', which includes as its main component the number of academic staff whose work was reported in the Exercise. The importance of the financial outcome on the one hand, and the grade on the other, varies between universities and departments. A similar contrast can be drawn in admissions work between the two aspects of the outcome (of new student registrations) *viz.* the actual number of students registered, and the school examination grades of the students admitted. Whereas both of these measures are important, their relative importance varies from case to case. It may be inappropriate to seek an entry group with the highest average grades, if that reduces the total entry below economic levels. (Needless to add that both these examples are simplified; there are other aspects of 'quality' which can be regarded as relevant, to varying degrees.)

Academics are inclined to seek the highest quality in all their activities, and along every dimension they can conceive. But if they are to prune their administrative activities, they need to focus on the relevant external quality criteria, and to apply the appropriate standards; moreover they need to resist the temptation to insist on high quality of other kinds.

Cutting out whole tasks

We have considered how to speed up the activities that make up an administrative task, and how to evaluate the component activities in the hope of finding some that can be cut out while still achieving the main goal of the task. The most ambitious form of cost-cutting in administration is to remove whole tasks – to give up whatever goals they were aimed at achieving.

Sometimes the very attempt to find its goal will reveal that some task was unnecessary. A prime candidate for surgery of this kind has been committee work, or rather, the work of some committees. In the 1980s many United Kingdom universities were subjected to a ruthless process of committee-pruning, and committees were removed from the structure where it was judged that their activities were superfluous to the functioning of the institution, faculty or department which they (supposedly) served. Some other candidates for surgery are:

- organizational structures in which activities are duplicated;

- documentary and information systems involving duplication.

- monitoring activities;

- maintaining archives and audit trails.

In academic life, it is often difficult to spot the difference between 'primary' productive activity and 'second-order' monitoring or checking – as examining students, or refereeing articles, form a necessary part of our 'primary' activity. But many colleagues would argue that United Kingdom universities have moved from a situation where there was (perhaps) too little scrutiny of our activity, to a situation where the demands made by the 'quality industry' for monitoring and inspection are excessive, and are displacing the primary activity of teaching and research.

Our next candidate for surgery is that of records, especially archives. Universities contain archivists, librarians, historians and other scholarly folk whose calling is to preserve records and documents for posterity. Without any disrespect to them, we observe that keeping every last piece of paper or computer file is not necessarily a good way of using scarce resources. Filing systems should have built-in decay periods so that documents that are kept are discarded at regular intervals. This sometimes is done, but not always. Another use of archives is to retain 'audit trails' not only for financial checking, but also (for example) to enable a department to trace the tutors of a student who, ten years after graduating, asks for a confidential reference. The value of retaining such information, storing it, and indexing it, needs to be set against the cost, which is often considerable. When resources are very scarce, some habits of retention may need to be broken. (We discuss this topic further in our chapter on paper-management, Chapter 8.)

Monitoring and archiving are activities that are additional to the primary processes of teaching and research. Our next two candidates for surgery arise from duplication. One motive of the many episodes of organizational restructuring that our universities have seen over the past fifteen years has been a search for 'economies of scale' where across an institution administrative tasks have been undertaken many times. Principles of collegiality and local autonomy tend to invite such duplication, and in more spacious times there were evident advantages. For example, in student admissions work, if a departmental admissions tutor handled all the applications from candidates for the department's degree programmes, and conducted the interviews, the long process of teaching and learning could begin with the admissions process itself, and suggestions for advance reading might be given in the interview. Also, an identification of the student with the teachers who would take them through the degree could start even before registration. Such admission processes are now a distantly-remembered luxury in many departments and universities, which have introduced centralized admissions processes and formula-based selection.

The progressive introduction and increased sophistication of computer-based information systems for administration promises to reduce duplication or to reduce the long-term cost of the task. A word of warning however on *short-term* costs. The myth of magical computerisation of chores dies hard, and is kept alive in universities by false analogies with what is done by banks or supermarkets. Two factors distance universities from such organizations, when it comes to the automation of administration. First, many universities are more loosely-structured as organizations, with autonomy vested in many component units such as academic departments or faculties. Second, the complexity of some of the central functions of academic administration, such as student registration in degree programmes and courses/modules, and tracking student progress through the years to degree classification, is greater than that of most data-management tasks in those other organizations. The extent of standardization between institutions is small, so that 'bespoke' solutions may be required for each university, although the cost of such solutions is high in relation to the budgets of individual universities. The labour which is involved in the designing, testing, and implementing of a new system, and the further effort that is required for training and supporting new users, is likely to entail a net increase in workload over several years before a new system will yield any savings at all on the time and effort account.

Our second form of duplication relates to items of information. The recording and storing of information takes (someone's) time, and effort, in creating and maintaining the storage system, whether they are hard-copy files and cards, or computerised databases. The ideal is to keep any needed information in a single but secure copy that is readily accessible to all who may have occasion to find it. Traditional paper storage methods did not make the ideal at all easy to achieve, at least not at any reasonable cost in time and effort (since a unique copy of a document would have to be read in a central library or store, or someone would have to be asked to find and read it, and pass the information back). Now electronic storage methods at least hold up the hope of just such economy in storage combined with ease of access.

Harmonizing the demands of all your tasks

Our approach to administration has, up to this point, been 'atomistic' – we have been considering administrative tasks one by one, to see how the time-cost of each might be reduced, even to zero in the most favourable cases. We have already noticed, however, that the timing of administrative demands gives an extra turn to the screw, as when periods that would have been de-voted to study or marking are interrupted.

When we have many responsibilities, both academic and administrative, it is a major challenge to harmonize their demands: to fit them together into a manageable pattern. To do this requires planning, and calls upon 'juggling' skills if we are to implement the plans as conditions change. Realistic anticip-ation of likely work-demands is called for. We need to take time to plan a period of work, indeed several nested periods (a year, a term or semester, a week, a day) to accommodate the various demands, while allowing for their particular requirements – place of work, time of day, availability of colleagues, library opening hours, etc. The most careful plans are apt to fail where tasks take longer than expected, or new demands supervene, hence the need to develop juggling skills – ways of keeping the threads of the various tasks in hand, and of recovering from interruptions.

➡️   ◀️

Summary of Chapter 6

This chapter has explained how varied are the tasks that are counted as 'administration'. It has examined the time management problems associated with these tasks, by considering the various activities that go to make them up. Three broad strategies for cutting down on administrative time are presented. A more radical approach is also considered, involving a review of an entire process. The many quality issues involved in administration are examined. Among types of administrative work, four candidates for removal are offered. The value of harmonizing different tasks is sketched.

➡️   ◀️

7 Time Management as a Research Project

This chapter considers time management as a worthy subject for research. It invites readers to draw on their own research skills and the knowledge gained in reading and acting upon previous chapters to plan and implement a course of action.

When you have read and acted on this chapter you will:

(1) know the nine key attributes of researchers that can be applied to time management problems;

(2) know the characteristics of a 'Master of Time';

(3) have a plan of action and know how to carry it out.

The challenge to manage time effectively is a problem that requires a solution.

So far we have explored the subject of time management in relation to the academic environment and offered some suggestions on how to deal with it.

In this chapter we offer an alternative and more general approach, developing a theme which we first introduced in Chapter 3. Time management is a legitimate subject for research. The kind of research which it requires necessarily has a personal dimension – the problem that can only be legitimately solved by individuals for themselves. In this chapter we invite you to draw on your own research skills, learning from the observations you have already been making about the way in which you may best improve your own responses to time-consuming demands. As such demands mount, developing your own defences may increasingly seem a condition of your survival as a competent or even as a sane person.

Since the problem of time management is brought about by the combined demands of teaching, research and administration, we need to mobilize all our professional skills to tackle it. Academics, being both teachers and researchers, have a distinct advantage over many other professions. After all, what is research if not an exploration of a problem and the formulation of some ways of handling it?

In the academic world degrees of Master and PhD confer on their owner the right of knowledge and mastery of a subject. After completing this course on time management, you can award yourself an MT ('Master of Time').

Although only *you* will be able to award yourself the MT, we shall be presenting in Chapter 11 some detailed criteria which will help you to decide how far you have gone in the mastery of the techniques of time management.

The project

For many academics it is the research, the creative thought, the thrill of discovery that makes academic life worthwhile. It is also research that informs our teaching. Here we invite you to embark on a personal research project, using the most important research instrument that we possess. As Beveridge (1950) puts it:

> the most important instrument in research must always be the mind of man.

What gives researchers the advantage is their mind-set. Researchers plan, organize and predict. Researchers can also run 'thought experiments' in their heads, before confronting a real-life test.

What are the principal attributes of researchers that make them so eminently suited to solving their own time management problems?

- Researchers analyse, design, explore, evaluate, synthesize.

- Having assessed the situation, researchers plan, assemble the necessary resources, and organize the course of their intended research.

- Researchers know that however hard and carefully they plan, things will inevitably change – researchers need to be flexible.

- Researchers know how to design controlled experiments, try them out and evaluate them.

- Using work that has gone before, researchers can design new experiments and modify them in the light of results.

- Researchers do not try just one method, they try several.

- Researchers are inquisitive, persistent and creative.

- Researchers have the ability to stand back and reflect on a situation.

The research method

In Chapter 3 we proposed the following research method:

(1) State the problem.

(2) Observe the situation.

(3) Reflect on and evaluate the situation.

(4) Plan a course of action.

(5) Carry out the plan.

(6) Monitor to see that the plan is carried out and what the effects are.

(7) Pause for review of activity, using the chosen measures or characterization of success/failure.

(8) Modify the plan.

(9) Repeat 5 to 8 as necessary.

We have already considered ways of stating the problem (in Chapter 3). Using Chapters 4, 5, and 6 you have observed your own situation. We have also invited you to begin the process of reflection and evaluation. Here are some further thoughts that may help you to take it further.

Reflecting and evaluation

When you have made your list of activities, look at it carefully and ask yourself questions such as:

Why are *you* carrying out these activities?

What is the goal of each activity?

What problems does your record reveal?

What relationships are there between the activities?

What are you doing that you would rather not be doing?

What are you failing to do that you wish you were doing?

Give yourself time to reflect

Bear in mind that creative ideas, research and problem-solving do not conform to strict timetables. Therefore, it is necessary to carve time out of an already overloaded schedule in order to have time to research the topic. To achieve control over time, it is a good idea to take out a little time each day, first to define the plan of the research and then to carry it out one piece at a time, thereby gradually beginning to assume control.

Planning a course of action

See this course of action as a three-stage process, each process below following as a consequence of the previous one:

(1) Plan to reduce the number of activities.

Ask yourself the following questions:

Can you cut the number of activities into something which is more manageable?

Are all the activities really necessary?

Are you in a position to re-negotiate your workload?

(2) Reduce the time taken by each remaining activity.

Ask yourself the following questions:

Can you cut down the time taken on particular tasks and contributions?

Do you need a change in methods in order to achieve this?

Are you applying standards which are higher than the task really needs?

(3) Reduce the total time by general re-organisation.

Ask yourself the following questions:

Can you change the relations between your own activities so that they might blend together more harmoniously?

Can you cut down the total time which is taken up by all your work?

Do you need to move demanding tasks to different parts of the day when you are at your best (or less demanding tasks to your 'low times')?

Do you know how long you can concentrate on a particular task?

Can you combine different activities together (to kill two birds with one stone)?

Do you apply the 80:20 rule? (The 80:20 rule – Pareto's Principle – predicts that you will complete 80 per cent of your tasks in 20 per cent of the time. Selecting that time, and the tasks for it, is therefore very worthwhile.)

Define and refine your plan

The next step is to define the current problem. You may see the problem as: 'I have ten jobs and I cannot see how all of them can get done in the time' or 'They are putting far too much work onto me' or 'I have far too much paper thrown at me by the administration and it is just piling up' or a mental block: 'I have no idea how I am going to do x, y, z'.

If you are someone who needs to move from 'they are piling too much on me' to 'I can control my work', two insights will help you to achieve this:

(1) One reason for my view of what they are doing to me is in *my response* to what is happening.

(2) I need to understand how I react, not simply in terms of the current task (the 'what'), but in terms of the way I respond to all tasks – my attitudes, skills, coping systems which include planning, scheduling, paper-management systems, interruption-restriction systems, and so on ('the how and the why').

The beginning of wisdom lies in seeing how something in yourself contributes to your suffering; and to locating that something, not in your response to a quite particular task, but rather in a larger pattern of activity and habits which have formed an unacknowledged backdrop to your response to the task in hand.

Your personal action-research model needs to provide a place for the notion of progress, along a continuum, using an iterative process; not just the notion of (one-off) achievement. This idea – the move from focus on product to focus on process – informs many of our suggestions. The kinds of problem that you are facing are so daunting to you that a once-for-all solution is not likely to be immediately available. A gradual build-up is required. Personal morale is much improved if you can characterize the problem in such a way that you can see that your response is getting better.

Goals are needed to inform short-term plans; they express the values that we care about. Because we rarely achieve even short-term objectives to the letter, we need to work with an iterative planning process. At every stage we have a clear long-term vision that informs our medium- and short-term plans. Should the last set of short-term plans fail, we go back to the drawing-board, and modify our plan, changing some of the goals, abandoning others. The goals are like the carrot dangling just out of reach that gets us moving forward. As we move, it recedes. No matter, as long as we are moving forward!

What should you change first? If your model offers the resources to conduct a cost-benefit analysis, you can start where it suggests a good benefit at low cost. Efforts should not be dispersed on too wide a front; as soon as one finds something significant it is best to concentrate on that aspect of the work. Even without the help of such a model, you can and should choose to focus on a single area of change – an area of maximum gain, where a first move can be completed quickly and can be expected to make a difference that matters to *you*. You may need to remind yourself that *no one* can do more than one thing at a time.

As with most undertakings, the success of an experiment depends largely on the care taken with preliminary preparations and the care with which it is carried out. Treat time management research in this way and it will succeed for you.

The characteristics of a 'Master of Time'

(Threshold criteria for the 'award of Master of Time'.)

When you have completed this course and your research project there are certain practical and behavioural criteria by which you can judge yourself – and which should also be detectable by third parties. The 'Master of Time' always:

> (1) in the personal control-room
>
> - places tasks and projects in order of priority;
>
> - forms plans and acts on them;
>
> - has a plan for *today*;

- crafts the day, the week, and those longer planning-periods, to fit in the various demands in the most economical and elegant way;

- maintains control-documents for projects and work areas;

- understands the flexibility of personal time;

- can both live with and use change and exploit each one of its opportunities.

(2) in the personal work-space (office, study, or workshop)

- keeps the place tidy;

- organizes the room functionally;

- uses paper-management systems;

- keeps paper up to date.

(3) out and about

- fulfils daily plans;

- meets deadlines, keeps promises;

- deals effectively with interruptions;

- keeps a diary to hand;

- uses meeting time wisely;

- is assertive (but not aggressive).

These criteria will be given again at the end of this course and will form part of your final assessment of yourself!

➡   ⬅

Summary of Chapter 7

This chapter has suggested that readers should research the subject of time management in the same way as they would tackle any research project. Attributes of researchers are listed. A research project is placed in the context of work towards the 'degree of Master of Time'!

➡   ⬅

---

8 Pushing the Paper

This chapter tackles a problem common to all academics whatever their subject area, namely, how to manage the paperwork. It reveals how you can keep track of your own paper and how you can manage documents as they flow across your desk.

When you have read this chapter you will:

(1) have considered ways of keeping track of your own paper;

(2) know how to classify papers for grouping and filing;

(3) have reviewed how a computer might help you in managing paper.

Are you pushing the paper, or is it pushing you?

Once upon a time there was no paper; once indeed there was no writing at all. The successive inventions of writing, and printing, and typewriting, and photocopying, and the fax machine, and word processing, have allowed what we are nowadays pleased to call 'hard copy' to develop a very vigorous life of its own. Paper piles up in our departmental pigeonholes; around our studies; on our shelves; and on any flat space above floor level that it can find to colonize. In that vast and extensive territory consisting of the horizontal surfaces in the rooms or offices occupied by academics in a university, paper holds sway. It is an awesome imperial power.

What is hidden in those piles of paper?

Only a Martian could describe things as we just did, surely? What the ignorant or cynical denigrate as mere piles of paper, are to us collections of *meaningful documents*: essays to be marked, notes for a lecture, copies of documentary source material, offprints of papers from colleagues, minutes of departmental meetings, letters from publishers, application forms from grant-awarding bodies, and so on, and on, and on. To be sure, the quantity of such documents is ever-increasing; and they do happen to be printed or written on paper; and the paper takes up space on desks, and shelves, sometimes even in filing cabinets. Admittedly keeping track of these documents gets harder all the time, as their number increases, and new varieties are continually evolving to populate every niche on our horizontal work-surfaces.

How could we possibly do without paper? Academics are prime *producers* of paper documents: articles, books, lecture notes, mark-sheets, reports on students, applications for research grants, promotion applications. Our principal form of expression, as researchers and teachers, lies in paper documents. Much of our administration is conducted using paper documents.

Time for paper

What is the relation between paper management and time management?

Dealing with paper takes time. Declan Treacy (1991) claims that the average office contains uncompleted paperwork that would require forty hours to clear. Paper is a primary tool of our work, but like other tools, it makes demands on us over and above what it takes to use it directly on the job. Paper needs to be stored and made accessible. Its physical characteristics place firm constraints on how it can be kept and handled. Managing paper presents an ever greater challenge as the total volume of paper documents expands, and as they come in greater variety.

The immediate use of paper documents consists of our reading them, and of our creation of new documents, whether by annotating old documents or producing fresh ones. In an episode of academic desk-work we will consult many documents, and create several more (from memoranda to letters to minutes to learned articles). The documents in current use contain the informational ingredients that we select from storage and use to concoct the next meal. We may compare the process of writing, or replying to an enquiry, to cooking; it transforms the information which we have gained from the documentary tools into the new dish that we serve up. And yet the informational larder remains fully stocked for future use – unlike a bag of flour, it is not exhausted even by repeated employment. (We are struck by the exception: the practice that one of our friends adopts of tearing out and discarding the pages, once read, of paperback novels. This treats a book as if it were a bag of flour. But the discarding is optional, even if as an approach to handling paper documents, it has much to commend it!)

If we compare paper documents with the utensils and ingredients in our kitchens, we note that the paper is physically far more uniform, and also that the number of documents we are called upon to keep in storage for future (and possibly repeated) consumption is far larger than the number of utensils and ingredients in the typical family kitchen. The physical uniformity of paper permits ease of storage in dedicated furniture such as paper-trays and filing cabinets, but also lends an unhelpful anonymity to paper documents, when compared with kitchen utensils, or with most commercially-obtained food ingredients with their distinctive packaging. (Printed books provide an instructive comparison, for they too are distinctively packaged, and provided only that they are shelved in their own dedicated furniture, bookshelves, are so much much easier to locate than are our papers when they are stacked in trays or files.)

Our special time-problems with paper documents come, not when they are ready to hand at the desk, but when they are out of sight – whether in piles, in trays, or in files stored in file drawers. Once an individual document is out of sight, we need either to remember where we put it, or to use some tracking system to ensure that when we do want it, we can find it. And since papers that are open to view also serve as reminders of those tasks we have not yet done, we need to employ some auxiliary means to remind ourselves to perform whatever task is associated with a paper, as soon as the paper reminder slips out of sight. Consequently we must spend time in storing papers systematically, and in noting down the tasks associated with them, together with some link to the place of storage. The more time we spend in this way, the less we need to spend in searching through piles, trays or files to find a wanted paper; and the less we regret failing to complete some task associated with a document we have hidden from sight and then forgotten.

The need to manage paper is derived from our need to find and to use it, or to remember it, where the quantity of paper exceeds what can conveniently and readily be kept in view on our desks or other working areas.

Processing paper documents

We control a *flow* of papers across our desks. Documents reach us by mail or by hand; we receive them and may hold them in a temporary store (in-tray or in-basket) before sorting them and immediately placing them in one of three locations:

- our working area

- a file

- the waste-paper basket

It is good to be strong-minded and at the first stage to consign every paper we can to the waste-paper basket. Papers that we may need to refer to at some future date, but which demand no immediate action, can be filed (we discuss filing systems later). We are left with papers that need some action before they can be discarded or filed. There are three other possible and final destinations for papers that have been dealt with at our desk:

- the post-box

- departmental out-tray

- person-post (employed when you return an essay directly to a student)

If we wish to retain several documents for current attention, we may need to create special holding areas close to our workspace: working trays. But it is very important not to allow current paper to accumulate in such a way that individual documents are not dealt with promptly, or lose their identities in anonymous piles. If you find that happening, there is an imbalance in your personal work-system. The hold-up is on the feeder-road on to the motorway represented by your desk. It needs to be dealt with by widening the feeder road (spending more time sorting and dealing with new papers, and discarding more of them or placing more of them directly in files) or by increasing the speed of traffic on the motorway (taking less time on individual items as they finally reach your desk, or spending more time at your desk dealing with working papers). Papers that are held back for action for several days should go directly into your main filing system, but there should also be a note of the relevant task and the place of filing on your agenda list.

We work so much with paper that a pile-up of 'incoming' paper is very likely to happen when we are suffering from total overload, that is, when the demands placed upon us exceed our capacity to meet them. Once this has happened, re-balancing our time between activities will not on its own match the problem, and we need to think of more radical surgery to cut down the demand. This topic was considered in Chapter 6 in relation to administration, and we return to it in Chapter 10 when we look for ways of tackling overload problems at their source.

Classification of working paper

How many working trays should you have, and what should each of them contain? Physical constraints will usually dictate a number between four and ten; and more than ten can strain your own working memory. The documents in a tray need to be dealt with continually, and the pile in each tray needs to be kept small, to reduce the risk of paper-loss. How should the paper be grouped into different trays as it flows in? How might you group

a student essay that you are to mark;

a pre-print of an article from a colleague in another university;

a departmental memorandum asking for opinions on the colour of paint to be applied to the corridor that goes past your room?

The first relates to one of the courses you are currently teaching; the second is loosely connected with one of your own current research projects, but also requires a response out of courtesy to your colleague; the third, if you decide to respond at all, invites a brief written response or perhaps a telephone call. In general, a document landing on your desk for consideration attaches itself to one or another *topic*; and invites a distinctive *action* from you.

Topic, and action, offer alternative classifications. If you classify entirely by actions to be taken, you might choose groupings such as:

■ reply directly;

- decide on opinion;

- get information, or opinions of others;

- read (for longer documents which need extra time);

- hold for next meeting of committee x.

As an alternative to the last item above, papers held for an event that will take place on a particular date (such as a committee meeting) could be kept in a separate 'tickler-file' numbered for each day of the month, with items in each day's slot that you plan to deal with on that day.

The disadvantage of 'action-based' groupings of current papers is that if we want the paper in a hurry, perhaps to answer a question from a colleague, we are likely to think of it in terms of its content, not of the action we had decided upon. If the stacks in our working trays are several documents deep, a 'creeping check' of all of them is tedious and time-consuming. The alternative grouping is by *content*: put the paper for each course you are teaching; each research project you are involved in; memos from your head of department, each in its own working tray. If you can readily divide your working paper into a handful of such categories, no more than (say) ten, this may be the best for you.

The ideal that these considerations suggest is a system combining both 'action' and 'content' categories: something like a mail-sorter, with rows and columns, so that every item is given both an action and a content classification. We can readily agree that anyone whose working paper is sufficiently voluminous and complex to require managing in this way should be requesting full secretarial support for his or her paper management, but that is not here assumed to be forthcoming. Mail-sorters tend to be expensive, and because each cell is of fixed size, they take up a lot of room, much of which is likely to be under-used.

Probably the most convenient way of grouping current working paper is by some combination of the two methods. If there is a steady influx of papers of a particular character, for example, essays to mark, give them their own tray. (Use removable labels on your trays so that as the demands change, you can convert a tray to another use.) If some action grouping is significant – you take 'reading' paper home each evening; you group items where you want to consult departmental colleagues – then use that. You can overcome the disadvantages of using what is essentially a one-dimensional grouping to satisfy the needs of a two-dimensional classification, by using such devices as removable coloured tags to distinguish between papers in the same tray. You can also use coloured plastic envelopes to provide groupings in one tray.

Storing documents: first principles

Unless you are fortunate enough to have a personal assistant who looks after *all* your paper (including course materials and research documents) you will have some way of storing documents yourself. The simplest possible is a single unstructured pile. This may be neat and tidy, or it may flow across the further reaches of your desk (see the account of 'the volcano theory of paper-management' below). If you add the latest accessions to the top of a single pile, perhaps starting a new pile when the last is one foot high, your pile is not unstructured at all, but rather ordered by date. Even so, it is likely not to be easy for you to find wanted papers, or to replace them in correct order if you remove them. Using a single stack of paper is consistent with ease of recovery only if you also index the papers as you add them to the stack. And in order to make removal and replacement possible, a pile would need to be placed on its side and supported in some way to stop the papers falling over. This is part of what a conventional filing system actually does.

As soon as you decide that although you need to keep papers, they must be in more than one pile, and preferably stored in such a way that you can find individual documents and return them to the same place without disturbing others, you are confronting some basic problems of paper-storage or 'filing'. If the very idea that you might have your own filing system sends shudders down your spine, we sympathize. We also believe that traditional filing 'systems' are often very tedious to use in relation to the benefits they may bring, and may even fail to produce the results you expected. But a few common-sense principles will go a long way to meeting most needs for systematic document-storage. These involve:

- physical considerations

- conceptual constraints

- practical principles

The volcano theory of paper-management (Lansdale and Edmonds, 1992)

Dr Schmidt, on appointment, was provided with a room, and a desk (with chair). The desktop was empty.

As tends to happen, Dr Schmidt received letters from academic colleagues, building societies, the central university administration, etc. He received copies of articles, drafts from his students, departmental meeting agenda papers and minutes. And so on. And so on.

As he received each document, he would read it at his desk. And then he put it down. When he had occasion to do some writing at his desk, he would push any papers away from the area immediately in front of him. As the number grew, he would pile the papers up – not only in front of him, but to the sides, indeed all around the space he kept for writing and for working on the document he was immediately concerned with. He used to bring his coffee and tea into his room, and placed the mug on the papers. Occasionally the mug would make a round stain, or he would spill the odd drop of coffee on some paper that happened to be lying there.

As papers were added – for he never took anything off the desk – the pile grew higher and spread to the back of the desk. (He did not stack papers in orderly piles, but rather higgledy-piggledy, overlapping one another.) Recent papers were always on top, so he could find them quickly. Also papers that arrived and were being dealt with at roughly the same time tended to stay together. He got to know what they looked like, and the occasional item of coloured paper, the occasional coffee stain gave some documents more of a personality of their own. And, as anyone would, he tended to remember what he was dealing with at about the same time as he was dealing with some of these more salient items.

So when someone came in and asked him about some matter mentioned in one of the learned articles that were nestling somewhere in his pile, usually he remembered something about the item – what time of year it was he first read it, or that he was thinking about it during a particularly boring meeting, and wasn't that the one just before Christmas when we were discussing the Christmas party venue? … and as he riffled through the pile he usually noticed some old friends among the papers, and knew he was getting warmer when, by one association or another, he felt he was in the right region and the right period.

Because Dr Schmidt never himself removed papers from his desk, the apparently disorderly pile formed a kind of mound, with a depression in the place next to his chair from which papers were removed to make space to write. The mound formed most of a circle, and fell off towards the edge of the desk. Something like two-thirds of a volcano, with the crater formed by the workspace in front.

As the pile grew, papers fell off the edge of the desk and were cleared away by the cleaners from the floor where they lay.

Physical considerations

These come from the shape, size and (lack of) rigidity of paper documents. Most documents you deal with nowadays will most probably be of A4 size (or American quarto), varying in thickness from one sheet to stapled or comb-bound documents up to 1cm thick. (A5-format booklets can be opened out to A4 size for conventional filing.) Rigid card containers (folders, envelopes, file-hangers) into which we place paper documents serve several functions:

(1) to hold floppy papers so that they do not fall over, or bend;

(2) to permit 'random access' to individual documents and their return to the same place in the sequence;

(3) to group related papers together;

(4) to provide a title area.

Conceptual constraints

As soon as we split our single pile of papers into two or more groups we need to have some principle to decide in which pile, or file, to put a document. We must classify documents, so that we know later which file to find them in. Most likely your research papers are already divided into groups on principles that you have used for many years. But as other papers pile up, you may need to invent new categories. Be assured that there is no objectively right way of doing this:

■ *Any* set of categories that enables you to classify a new document, and to find it again in the place you put it, fulfils the only function that such a 'classification system' has.

The categories or concepts which you employ to group papers should be usable both for sorting new papers, and for finding and re-filing old ones: that is all!

Most such categories will grow naturally from the subject-matter you are dealing with. Correspondence can be grouped by the sender, or if from yourself, the recipient. Teaching materials can be grouped by course, and within course as (perhaps) student essays, material you hand out, your own background notes, and so on. If you are a member of one or more committees, papers for each committee can be kept together. If in doubt, follow the archivist's rule that we have already used in sorting correspondence: file documents by source (and if they originated with yourself, by destination).

Practical principles

We recommend 'files not piles' because piles are difficult to manage, they gather dust, they are hard to label, and they effectively preclude random access or later replacement. But what kind of files to choose? There are many alternatives, including box files, filing cabinets with hanging files, rotary systems and lateral shelf-filing systems.

In spite of what you see in office furniture catalogues we would urge that uniformity is not a virtue when it comes to filing systems.

Most academics are very familiar with one 'filing system' for documents, when the documents are printed books: the bookshelf. This item of technology matches the physical characteristics of books, which come all ready to be shelved, with their spines displaying their identity and individuality. Publishers use a variety of colours, textures and typefaces on the spines of their products to individuate volumes. We find familiar books on our own bookshelves more quickly because we know what they look like, and because there is variety in colours and styles.

We recommend that you think of files as like books. Ideally, each file would be as distinctive, and as salient to the viewer, as a single book. Needless to say, this ideal is not generally supported by the manufacturers of filing systems, who regard uniformity as a virtue.

The most familiar filing hardware, the filing cabinet with hanging file-drawers, compounds anonymity with invisibility, since when the drawers are closed the file-labels cannot be seen. In practice, for frequent users, the contents of such cabinets come to acquire individuality because the spatial configuration remains stable and the user gradually learns where individual files are to be found – as when a book is recalled mainly by its (usual) location on one's bookshelves, rather than by the colour of its spine.

Time is saved as we get up to speed in using the system. This happens more quickly when we have ourselves created the locations for new files. (I remember where *I* put something better than I remember where *you* put it because in my own case 'factual' memory –whether propositional or pictorial – is aided by 'motor' memory.) In both cases, book and file, alphabetical ordering is usual, and an alphabetical range can be marked on the file-drawer label.

An alternative to the conventional filing cabinet is a shelf-filing system, which comes close to offering the advantages of book-shelving but for paper documents. Box-files for their part mimic the format of large books, but they may be too high for many bookshelves. (There is a disadvantage too in that they take up the same space whether they contain one sheet of paper or two hundred sheets, and as a result may be wasteful of space.)

Using more than one storage style – perhaps a mixture of conventional filing cabinets and box-files – will give both more variety and distinctiveness and will therefore make locations of particular papers that much easier to remember. Some labelling systems also offer a variety of colours which can help to lend particular files or drawers some measure of individuality.

Another factor to consider in choosing a filing system – if you are in a position to make that choice – is *flexibility*. Some of the older systems use file-hangers that are attached to one another in series, and this makes inter-polating a new file in alphabetical sequence very tedious, compared with a system which treats each file-hanger or folder independently. Ease of titling and re-titling is another aspect of flexibility.

What about information technology?

Can computers help us to manage paper? Better still, can they help us to manage *without* paper?

Twenty years ago, when word-processors (the 'dedicated' variety) were first invading office workplaces, the 'paperless office' was confidently pre-dicted. By today, when most clerical and administrative offices have been using computers for word-processing for at least ten years, and spreadsheets and computerized databases are also in widespread use, we know that the early predictions have not been fulfilled. The rate of generation of paper documents has increased, not diminished.

'Word processing' has always been principally a mode of production of paper documents – the computer as a superior typewriter. The other most familiar office applications for computers, namely spreadsheets and data-bases, are more distinctively computer-based, and there is structure in the computer file that cannot readily be represented on paper, nor seen on a single screen. With the advance of computer networks, electronic mail has also become common in the workplace.

E-mail has displaced paper correspondence for many purposes, and most users will not feel the need to print out every message, or to send an e-mail message text in hard copy as well. Whether this has reduced the total volume of paper mail is more questionable, as the total volume of mail of all kinds has increased many times. Spreadsheet and database work on computers may have displaced some non-computer work; but the increase in facilities and sophistication of computer financial models, database systems and suchlike has added new functions as well.

When the documents we work with are received or created, and stored, on computers, document-management problems for computer users arise that are very similar to the paper-management problems we have been discussing. These are quite separate from the uses of computers to ease the paper-management problem. But we turn to those first.

Computer-assisted paper-management

If you are dealing with large volumes, or a large variety, of paper documents, you may find some help in using one or another computer program. We pointed out above that papers above a bare minimum in volume or variety require us to develop *auxiliary links* between individual documents and ourselves in our work-spaces. The intermediate links are the file titles that identify the groups into which we have sorted our documents; and the notes of tasks that are associated with particular documents that we have nonetheless consigned to a file to hold them out of the way until we are able to deal with them. A computer might be used to create and hold

a catalogue of file titles;

an index of documents;

a list of tasks and associated documents.

Our file titles can be listed in a *catalogue*, indeed this is commonly done in clerical offices, so that the locations of the various files can be noted and the information shared among various users. An *index* is an altogether more ambitious affair, being a list of all documents with their file-labels and locations. If you are a scholar or archivist you will probably use such an index of any source materials you hold, or of your collection of offprints and photocopies. But you are unlikely to wish to maintain an index of other papers. Even a catalogue is more trouble than it is worth if your system extends to no more than fifty file hangers. The third type of list associated with your filing system is the one that associates *tasks* on your personal agenda with *documents*.

Lists are, to the computer, text files or database tables. Lists of the kind we have just mentioned can readily be stored in the simplest of computerised 'flat-file' or 'card-index' systems, with advantages in editing, and searching, compared with a physical card-index system, for example. Keeping such lists even as word-processed files would have many of the same advantages. Contemporary computer applications provide many similar features in this area; the program which you know best is likely to be the most efficient for you. (Remember that installing and learning a *new* computer application is itself costly in time.)

Document-management for computer users

If you are using a computer to create documents, or to receive them (as e-mail messages, for example) you will have many of the same needs for computer file-management as we all have for paper document-management. (A 'file' to the computer is what a 'document' is to the paper-user; at the next level, a 'folder' or 'directory' to the computer is what a 'file' is to the paper-user. The explanation for this confusion of terminology is historical.) E-mail systems usually provide holding areas for incoming messages, without our needing to create them. Once messages have been read, they may be stored or discarded; and as with paper documents, discarding should be the preferred option unless you are clear in your mind that you want to keep a copy. Your e-mail system, until you tell it otherwise, will almost certainly keep all the e-mail messages that you store in a single pile (folder/directory). But it should permit you to create a separate folder for different groups of messages, for example, messages to or from the same correspondent. This is as useful and necessary in keeping track of computer files as it is for paper documents.

The same principles apply to storage of documents that you create yourself, whether using a word-processor or some other program. Such 'applications' will usually come set up to store new documents in the same folder as the program itself, but this is not a desirable system. Create a folder or directory for each area or topic on which you work, and store in it all the files associated with that topic, whether word-processor files, spreadsheets or database files. (The programs – applications – will have no difficulty in detecting their own files; there is no danger that they will accidentally load a file from another program.)

Just as we keep precious documents in lockable filing cabinets, it is worth thinking how to protect valued computer files. The ease of copying computer files means that protecting them from either accidental or malicious damage is also easy – as long as you remember to do it, or install an automatic backup system to do it for you. Never keep valued documents in single computer copies, even on floppy discs that you remove from the computer. If you use a networked computer, it may be that files stored on network drives are archived by your system managers daily, or weekly; but you need to confirm this, do not take it for granted. Computers as physical systems are subject to breakdown or theft that can remove or destroy data stored on hard discs. The data stored in them is also vulnerable to virus attack, which is commonplace in universities and can result from moving data using floppy discs or from files downloaded from the Internet. Use an up-to-date virus-checker and ensure that your material is well backed-up. (The time this will take is like an insurance premium – a little but often, and out of all proportion to the time that you would lose if valued documents were lost or corrupted.)

Computerised document-management?

Some commercial organizations are much closer to having paperless offices than are most universities. Hard-copy documents can be rendered into electronic form using scanners, which enable computers to store facsimiles or to record structured data that was formerly kept in hard copy. As scholars will be aware, documentary archives are also now available in electronic form, whether in facsimile or as text-files. But a wholesale move away from use of paper documents to electronic formats does not seem likely in universities, even for administrative purposes, for several years yet. The commercial organizations (such as insurance companies) that have already achieved this are tightly-controlled and use a comparatively small number of data formats. They also have large information technology budgets and are more 'capital-intensive' than universities, where (we academics are happy to note) most 'core' teaching and research tasks will continue to require a significant 'labour' input for the foreseeable future.

Summary of Chapter 8

Documents are the very stuff of our work, and paper is still a dominant medium. To keep up with the heavy flows of paper into our working spaces, we need to give some time to designing and using systems for controlling and storing paper documents. A few common-sense principles that respect the physical form of these documents, and our own needs in storing them, will go a long way towards dealing with the paper problem.

9 Working with Other People

This chapter reviews the social context of time management in academic life. Academic colleagues, our other co-workers and our students can help us or hinder us in managing time. Some of our tasks are social by their very nature, and present special challenges for those who would use time wisely.

When you have read and acted on this chapter you will:

(1) understand the importance of human relationships for time management;

(2) be able to enlist the support of others in managing your time, and to avoid or defuse social situations which threaten to waste time;

(3) understand the value of social forms of work, and how to make them productive without taking too much time.

The importance of human relationships

For the majority of us, effective time management requires control over our social activities and relationships. This is most obviously the case where our work activity has a directly social character, such as in team-work, in meetings, in conversations or in correspondence. But our relationships with other people affect our actions in many ways even outside such social activities.

Both in teaching and in research, we are usually working with an audience in mind – a student group, the editor of a learned journal, a conference session. Our perception of the audience's demands and our understanding of the expectations of colleagues, influence the standards we adopt, and therefore the time we take – even in work that we do alone.

Then there are the more annoying influences of other people – from trivial interruptions when someone knocks at the door or the telephone rings, to disputes and feuds which can absorb immense amounts of our time once we get caught up in them, including time drawn from other activities if the problems tug at our attention. Even the minor interruption, if it derails a train of thought, can have a quite disproportionate effect on the value of a period set aside for concentrated reading.

Skill in time management calls upon social skills. But the professional training or 'formation' of most academic staff has been individualistic – there has usually been little or no emphasis on social skills even for those who have successfully completed a doctorate.

We want others to be working with us, not against us, as we seek to manage our time. We want our social activities to be conducted in such a way as to make the best use of the time available. And we want our relationships to support, rather than to threaten, the management of our own time.

Working with others on time

Other people can undermine our attempts to get control of time, but other people can also provide excellent support. We have to find out in what ways we can get other people to help in our time management and also how we can prevent them from hindering it.

The first step is to achieve a shared understanding of the importance of time, and an acceptance that time-considerations are relevant to all activity. This may not be easy. The habit of treating time as a 'free good' dies hard. But it is a basic element in good management to count the cost of any new activity, and to assign adequate resources to it. Where the resource is someone's time and effort, good management requires that this must be taken into account just as financial resources are. It has to be accepted that time is a strictly limited resource.

The value of time should become a common concern in your working group. One way of putting it on the group's agenda is to arrange for a short time management course to be attended by all the staff in the unit.

Support for individual time management

In our effort to achieve this we should first of all look at ways in which other people can be enlisted in support of one's own moves towards better time management, such as:

- not interrupting

- giving good notice

- meeting deadlines

- being punctual

- doing things right first time

- arranging helpful timetables

- accepting 'delegated' tasks

- collaborating to achieve economies of scale

Others can be asked to help us by *not interrupting*, when we are engaged in kinds of work which would be severely disrupted even by short breaks. You may be able to switch the telephone through to a secretary or to your answering machine, to post a 'Do not disturb' notice on the door, to take your examination marking home and leave the telephone there off the hook. Such arrangements are best agreed with colleagues wherever possible, and are easier to sustain if they are reciprocated – if we are prepared to do unto others as we would have them do unto us. Where secretarial support is not available to answer the telephone, for example, some colleagues have pairing arrangements so that one answers the telephone in the morning, the other in the afternoon, and each takes messages for the other.

Others help us, and we help them, by *giving good notice* of requirements for reporting, and by producing papers by the deadlines that have been set. It has been a feature of the increased pace of academic life, combined with galloping bureaucracy, that more and more forms and reports are now being required with ever-shorter deadlines. These changes have increased the stress of academic work, and they have also reduced the efficiency of time-use, because they make planning so much more difficult, and tend to introduce interruptions which reduce overall effectiveness and raise the total time-cost of the activities they have interrupted.

If *deadlines* are not met, and someone has to chase up missing reports, whoever is doing the chasing has extra work. Such additional work is not productive; it is a net increase in total workload that has no positive effect whatsoever. Sometimes we find it necessary to chase up replies because we have had no acknowledgement of receipt of the original request. Not only in universities, the practice of sending acknowledgements, however brief, of letters and other communications has all but died out. But a minimal acknowledgment, even a pre-printed card (or a one-line note sent by e-mail) can save time all round.

Simple *punctuality* – in arriving at appointments of any kind – saves time in much the way that meeting deadlines does. If you and I have an appointment at a certain time, and you pause from an activity to be ready for it, but I arrive ten minutes late, during that time you may not be able to start a new activity, or make effective use of the indeterminate period of waiting. Predictability of commitments makes for good time management; the unpredictable takes a toll. The value of punctuality is multiplied many times in meetings with several people – whether these are classes, or committee meetings, or any large gathering. It is not just bad manners, but very costly in time to arrive late for such occasions when you are part of the *quorum*, as the time of those who arrive on time is almost certainly not being used to best effect while they wait for you.

Others can help us too, as we can help them, by *doing things right first time*. In many areas of academic work, standards are important, indeed are of the very essence of the activity (as in examination marking). In such cases we have systems that check the accuracy of results, or review marks. In such cases too there is a conflict between ensuring that standards are observed, and reducing the time-cost of the activity. Sometimes a modicum of extra care over the first marking – perhaps involving writing brief comments on individual scripts – can allow for a much lighter checking process, so reducing time-costs all round. ('Second-marking' can be replaced by 'monitoring'; see Chapter 4.) But we academics also need to remember that not all activities need to be performed to the high standards that we set for publication in international journals. We need to be sensitive to what is 'good enough' – so 'right first time' means only, 'good enough first time', not 'perfect first time'. The production of documents is a rewarding field for applying this. Most of us are pedants about certain matters close to our subject interests; and rightly so when we are marking student work, or vetting material for international journals. But where we are communicating with colleagues on general matters, the extra time it takes to ensure (what we take to be) good style, factual accuracy, full documentation, adequate proof, has to be weighed against consideration of the minimum standard demanded by the context. And when we are writing minutes, internal memoranda, and other administrative communications, it is well to remember how little of such material is actually read carefully, or even (by some) at all. A short and telegraphic note, with no more than half a dozen 'bullet points', is more likely to be read and digested than is a 5,000-word diatribe.

How effective our use of whole days, weeks and semesters is, depends in part on the *timetable* for our teaching commitments and the other fixtures in our diaries. As individuals we can and should seek to negotiate with the timetablers schedules that enable us to make the best use of all our time. For some of us this will mean bunching teaching commitments into the minimum number of days per week in order to free time for preparation, marking and research without frequent changes of gear into teaching mode, or having to clear working areas repeatedly for student use. For others this may mean grouping teaching commitments into a particular time of day. If you find it hard to get on with research without a full day being dedicated to it, then – provided that research is part of your duties – you may be able to negotiate with your timetablers certain ways to protect a day in the week for that, even during teaching terms.

Others can help us by doing some or all of our work for us. That is, we can and should (where possible) *delegate*. Many works on time management mention delegation as a standard technique, but they also tend to assume that the reader has a secretary or personal assistant – and we dare to make no such assumption here. However, delegation 'down the line' is not the only way of arranging for others to do one's work. Our example of telephone-swapping hints at another way – 'sideways delegation'.

It is well worth considering too whether there are any *economies of scale* that could be achieved in your working group. An example from the area of research is in finding suitable journals at which to target particular articles, or finding suitable grant-awarding bodies to which to apply for support for a new research project. In some research teams and departments forms of collaboration and sharing of information already exist to minimize the labour involved in such activities. A modest investment in meetings of colleagues, and setting up good internal communications (such as e-mail lists) can pay off handsomely. Solutions of this kind are now almost forced upon us by the 'information explosion' which involves a continuing information *inflation*, as sources proliferate, items of information become ever more numerous, and yet individual scholars and researchers are still required, in order to meet professional standards, to track all available sources. A contemporary example (as we go to press) is the increase in information on the Internet, which is forever running ahead of the capacity of World Wide Web searchers and other secondary systems to track new information and to index it in a usable form.

Another area for seeking economies of scale within a department is in teaching: specifically, in the sharing of information about teaching methods. University teachers are having to cope with increasing numbers of students, and there are innovative teaching methods in use that are directed to achieving more effective use of staff time. But also, many of us are used to having complete individual responsibility for our teaching methods, and may not think of turning even to immediate departmental colleagues for ideas on coping with larger numbers. Once again, a modicum of investment in the sharing of information can lead to long-term economies in time and effort.

A source of pressure against sharing intellectual tasks comes from our sense of our own intellectual property rights, and the concern to avoid any form of plagiarism. It may be necessary to reflect where such considerations apply, and where they do not. If we publish over our own name, the work should indeed be our own, and is most certainly subject to rules forbidding plagiarism. But it is not obvious that exactly the same rules apply to material presented in lectures or classes, where these are presented on behalf of the department. If a course has been well-presented and moreover documented by a colleague who is not available to teach it this year, it may and perhaps should be the norm rather than the exception for the next teacher of that course to take over much of the 'courseware' without troubling to re-write the entire course. And in matters administrative, we would do well to accept working systems when we take over an established role.

Meetings and other conversations

Some tasks can be eased by collaborating with others. Other tasks are by their very nature collaborative. From an informal two-person conversation to the most august and tradition-bound meeting of a university governing body, our work involves social activities. And as soon as two or more people are gathered together at the same time to perform some task, the total time-cost rises. How long does it take you to prepare a new lecture course, or to write an article? Typical answers will be in the tens of hours, just possibly topping

100 hours. A 2-hour meeting of a fifty-person senate uses up 100 hours of time in the meeting room (even leaving travel times out of account). As time is increasingly pressured and *should* be increasingly valued, we need to be very sure that meetings are needed; and that the meeting time is well-used.

What else, apart from prompt starting, with all members present, promotes the effective use of time in meetings? There is the matter of the ending-time. Some meetings, such as lectures, have a fixed terminus. Others are open-ended, but often with local traditions that say that a committee meeting is not expected to last more than 90 minutes, for example. In the more formal university bodies, there may be standing orders governing the duration of meetings, even if they are rarely invoked. A clear contract about the finishing time between the chairman or woman of a meeting and its members is desirable. Then there is the use of the time between the start and the end. Lecturers learn to pace themselves and not to defer half the content they wish to convey until the last few minutes of a 50-minute lecture. Staff who chair meetings carry a heavy responsibility for the effective use of time, often having to deal with conflicting demands for the use of the precious 'air-time'. And every member who would speak has some part of the responsibility for the good use of the time of all the members present.

An effective period of study requires concentration, and similarly so does an effective meeting. The topic of discussion should be focused and sustained, and contributors should not ramble away from the point. Meetings need a purpose, and it helps if the purpose or purposes can be stated and agreed early on, and for the subject of each phase of discussion to be made clear. These are the functions served by a printed agenda in more formal meetings.

Time management and relationships

'Relationships' form a constantly evolving background to our passing social encounters with individuals and groups. The term covers the roles and responsibilities that shape these encounters, but also the more personal aspects: relations that are friendly or hostile, trusting or mistrustful, and so on. The character of our working relationships, indeed of all our personal relationships, has a pervasive effect on our use of time. To take one example: if we *trust* colleagues – to keep their promises, or to do a job well – we are far likelier to feel happy about asking them to undertake some task for us, thus lightening our own load, than if we distrust them. And another: if there is a relationship of hostility between two colleagues, the effectiveness of their collaboration is threatened, and with it the scope for mutual support in time management.

For some of us, some of the time, developing relationships is directly part of our jobs. All teachers need to develop a relationship with their classes; this feature is at its most prominent in one-to-one teaching situations, such as individual tutorials and graduate supervisions. Many of us also have forms of responsibility for other staff, for example in the context of staff review systems. And some have direct personnel responsibilities, as heads of department, or leaders of research teams.

If relationships are good, then mutual support in time management is just one of the many benefits we can enjoy; and if relationships are sour, not only is effectiveness challenged, but in the worst cases all efforts at control of time may be derailed. If we find ourselves embroiled in a feud, or if we become convinced that other colleagues are trying in some way to undermine our position, we may become so involved in dealing with the problem and in brooding about it that work on other tasks is sabotaged. Our capacity to control our own activities and to manage our time is always affected by our emotions and by the atmosphere in which we work. Poisoned relationships can hijack our emotions, or sour the atmosphere.

A moral of all this is that time spent on developing good working relationships, and time spent on dealing with interpersonal difficulties or conflicts, is not necessarily time wasted, even if it is taken from our 'primary' activities of teaching and research. In the longer run our ability to use time well in primary activities is dependent in good part on the quality of our relationships, so time spent on developing and sustaining them is time well-invested, whereas ignoring them is perilous, even if it appears to save time in the short run.

How to avoid or defuse social situations which threaten to waste time

Unwanted interruptions can be avoided by some of those stratagems which we mentioned earlier, such as posting 'Do not disturb' notices; using an answering machine or switching the telephone through to a colleague or secretary (by prior agreement); finding a workplace out of reach of interruptions ('hiding in the Library'). However, keeping a balance between valued contact with colleagues and time-wasting is difficult. Rationing your appearances in the coffee-room may be advisable. If you need to accept callers, but find that some appointments run on out of your control, consider meeting in the other person's room, so that you can leave when it suits *you*.

It is always much easier to prevent interruptions than to terminate a conversation once it has started. Some people find it very hard to extricate themselves even from simple and informal conversations; others seem to manage to terminate even the most demanding ones. There is no substitute for developing some social skills to deal with difficult situations. Just one short course on assertiveness, or on handling conflict, may help to suggest some ways in which the more difficult encounters can be controlled and, when necessary, terminated. A surprisingly good way of terminating a conversation is simply to walk away; and if that is not possible, simply to fall silent. Such techniques are mainly of use when the other person is being manipulative, and is trying to recruit you to some cause, or otherwise to engage your attention against your better judgment. (Such manipulative techniques are by no means confined to doorstep evangelists and vendors of second-hand cars!)

What work, anyway?

We must get the division of labour right. In teamwork, when we share work out or 'delegate' downwards or sideways, different people do different things. Separation and differentiation of roles is normal in working groups. This reflection reminds us of the curious blend of team-working with individual entrepreneurism that characterizes academic life. In research, forms of teamwork are the norm in laboratory sciences, but are the exception in the humanities, the social sciences, and mathematics. In teaching it is usual for us to take individual responsibility for a course or module, but to collaborate in planning whole degree programmes. But first year courses or modules using new technology are nowadays often taught, or 'managed', by more than one person. On the other hand it is quite common for one teacher/researcher to be the sole accredited expert in their specialism within the university that employs them. When it comes to administration, we recognize that administrative roles taken by academics can be passed around the department – and in so doing, we implicitly allow them the status of 'generalist' jobs; but at any one time, these roles are likely to be filled by a single individual.

Good teamwork and effective distribution of tasks in a working group require that as far as possible jobs are done by people who are able to do them with the least effort. They also require that individuals who may be better than others at tasks needed by the whole group are rewarded and recognized for their contribution to the total work of the group. The current funding environment of United Kingdom universities militates against a rational distribution of labour, but within the existing limits the importance for time management of such a distribution needs to be recognized, and to be acted upon as far as is possible.

Workload allocation systems

Many academic departments have arrangements for dividing up the work of teaching. (In some cases, individuals' total loads have been set by national agreements; in others, such matters are left to institutions or to departments.) Increasingly, in the context of ever-higher demands on time, these systems have been developed to encompass administrative and research commitments. There are several different models, but usually the measures employed involve a mixture of 'input' and 'output' criteria. (From the point of view of the individual member of staff, countable 'inputs' might include contact hours; whereas such items as the number of students who complete a course, or the number of articles or books which are accepted for publication, count as 'outputs'.) To the extent that such systems reflect the personal cost of a particular workload, they can be used to apportion work fairly among members of staff.

If individuals are allowed to negotiate their workloads from year to year, a workload allocation system may allow them to undertake additional non-research work in one year in order to buy more research time in the next. So access to decision-making can become part of the individual's armoury in managing work-time from year to year. Such systems can also help us in time management if they define clearly the total responsibilities of the individual members of staff, who can then plan their duties without fear that additional tasks will be imposed without notice or without recompense.

Workload allocation systems have to operate within the context of the total demands on the department or unit. If the external resource system is hostile – if funding per student is being reduced, whereas the cost in time and effort of teaching each student is roughly constant – such a system can do nothing to improve the overall situation. The best it can do is to apportion the work equitably, leaving the problem of coping with increasing workloads still to be addressed.

The value of social forms of work

Working with others is not always easy. It often seems to us (as a character in Sartre's *Huis Clos* wryly observes) that 'Hell is other people'. Managing time is easier for a hermit than for someone working in a team. From one individual's point of view, other humans may appear mainly in the role of impediment rather than support. At a theoretical level, we may recognize our dependence on others, but in their day-to-day work many academics would often prefer to be able to work in solitude ... except when we need the unfailing support of a secretary, a librarian, someone from the computer centre, or of another member of our research team!

We would do well to remember that publication is one form of communication, and that communication is a social activity. Teaching is another form of communication. Notwithstanding famous examples of 'hermit' academics who have been 'non-publishers', teaching and research gain their value only within a social dimension. We became teachers and researchers ourselves only at the behest of others (who taught us and certified our competence). Administration too is primarily a social activity, even when the media of communication are application or report forms, or involve 'meetings, bloody meetings'. Where social activity is intrinsic to our work, we have no choice but to make the best of it, whether we find it rewarding or not.

Administration often involves making decisions that are jealously retained within the academic arena. This may be because the content involves 'peer-assessment', for example the assessment of individuals for higher doctorates; or because the principle is 'collegial' and some non-academic decisions are regarded as the proper province of the academic department or senate. In such cases, the social activity involved in the decision-making is (to that extent) highly valued, and the time-cost represents the price we pay for holding back the tide of 'managerialism'. But we can still guard against unnecessary costs.

Summary of Chapter 9

This chapter has looked at the social context of time management in academic life. We noted the importance of sharing an understanding of the value of time among the members of a working unit or department. Ways of helping others to help us manage time were reviewed: punctuality, predictability, giving notice, keeping documents short. The importance of sharing and of distributing work was considered, and opportunities for making economies of scale were noted. We also noted how the quality of our relationships with others influences our use of time.

10 Tackling the Problem at its Source

This chapter considers the need to say 'no'. There are personal limits to the amount of work that one can accomplish in 24 hours and for health and sanity overload must be contained. Ways of stemming the flood of demands on us are considered.

When you have read and acted on this chapter you will:

(1) have considered the need to say 'no' in the context of your own work;

(2) know why a limit should be set on the amount of time we spend on work in terms of health and time for family life;

(3) have considered and acted on three proposals for stemming the flow of demands on your time.

The need to say 'no'

In order to take control of our time and our work if we have lost it, and to stay in control once we have regained it, we need to be able to contain the total demands on our time. For an academic saying 'no' it is sometimes an easy matter, but more often, it is somewhere between quite difficult and impossible.

A student asks you for advice on a topic you know little about, but on which one of your colleagues is the departmental expert; you gratefully direct him or her to your colleague. The staff appointments' office telephones you to ask if you are able to serve on an appointing committee on a certain date; unfortunately your diary is already full for that day, so you gratefully decline. In either of these cases it comes easily to say 'no'. Even in these cases, your saying 'no' does not (usually) make the work disappear from the agenda, it just moves it from one person's agenda paper to another's, and in the process may take up more of the time of the person who issues the request (in our examples here, the student, or the administrator in the staff appointments' office).

In some matters you are free to say 'no' without in any way infringing either your contract of employment, or past commitments to colleagues. You are free to turn down an invitation to review a book, or to act as an external examiner for a subject department in another university. In such cases as these, the work will pass to another, at the cost of additional work on the part of the person who is inviting you to act; but there is at least the possibility of some cost to yourself in turning down the request. Academic reputations are built in part upon the minor publications such as book reviews. Our standing among our professional colleagues in our national subject groups does depend upon the kind of response we give to invitations to provide such services as external examining, and a record of such activity is usually taken into account (among many other elements) in the promotion exercises of our own universities.

Saying 'no' to a new administrative imposition within our own department (or research unit) is another matter. Now the costs come close to home, since if the job has to be done, it will be done by one of our immediate colleagues. We may not be free to turn down such 'offers', if our department has a framework of workload-allocation including administrative chores in which all members of staff have to take their share. Accepting reasonable impositions within such a framework is likely to be part of our contracts of employment. We assume that when saying 'no' threatens our continued employment, this form of time-protection is becoming altogether too costly. If the total workload we are asked to undertake seems unmanageably large, notwithstanding our efforts to organize and to streamline our work, then some other means must be found of getting its scale under control. (To give up at this point may involve applying for early retirement, or 'downshifting', provided only that you are able to take retirement, or to re-negotiate your contract in order to work in a less demanding environment.)

Many of the demands upon us that we should most happily decline, or reduce in scale, are also those which it is hardest to cut without vigorous negotiation with authorities and bodies at higher levels. For example, we may find ourselves subject to bureaucratic demands in the conduct of our teaching activity that are costly in time and effort, such as requirements to audit colleagues' lectures and seminars, to complete complex reports on our own courses, to produce new and extensive documentation for students. Such demands may arise from university or faculty rules and regulations that have usually been set up to meet external impositions reflecting views of what counts as adequate 'quality monitoring'. To say 'no' to such demands, or to enter into negotiation to reduce them, involves activity at departmental level or above, in the individual university, even perhaps collectively at the national level, addressed to the funding agencies and government departments from whence such demands ultimately emerged.

In the example just given, there are many academics who believe that such activities in the name of 'quality' are worthwhile, and that they even tend (in the better cases) to raise the general standard of teaching. This is not in question here. As long as such activities represent a cost in time and effort, reducing them would (to that extent) reduce our total workloads. For the most part we may assume that our workloads consist of activity which *is* productive of good teaching and research. So if those workloads are excessive, reducing them will involve *some* cost in the quantity or quality of our work. (If we were to abandon all book-reviewing, this would reduce the quality of research work by cutting off an important source of information and opinion about recent publications.)

We do not suggest that saying 'no', or 'not so much' is cost-free; we do suggest that if the total costs of *never* saying 'not so much' are clearly unacceptable, this too must be placed in the balance. We are familiar enough with this mode of thinking when the issue is *money*; always there will be items that we should like to own, and services that we should like to enjoy, but for which we do not have adequate financial resources. What we are less familiar with, both as individuals and as members of decision-making bodies, is treating our time and effort as a 'scarce resource' in the way that we treat money; as a resource that is strictly limited.

We are not in the habit of counting the cost *in time and effort* of our plans and projects. Even if we were to try to estimate that cost, we would find it difficult to do so, because so much of our work is non-routine, or is being tried for the first time (as happens in periods of rapid change in methods and procedures).

When is it simply too much?

If the demands on us rise without limit, then clearly something will give way. The outer limits of acceptable workload are set by such considerations as the following:

- Each of us is subject to a *personal upper limit* beyond which any attempt to do more will be counter-productive, because beyond this point, our total 'output' will actually drop. This is expressed by the outer and downward track of the 'human performance curve' (Sutherland and Cooper, 1990).

- We have a *right to a private life*, to a family life, to some waking time on personal projects (even to keep up with the mundane necessities of existence: getting ourselves housed, clothed and fed, paying bills, attending to basic maintenance); and so a right to limit our total working time in such a way as to allow for these activities.

- We have a *right to health* – and so a right to contain the demands (and stresses) of work to ensure that our health is not threatened. This requirement, like the first, also sets a cut-off point beyond which additional work is simply counter-productive. When protracted or chronic illness supervenes, our capacity for work is reduced and may (for a time) be suspended completely.

The personal costs of overload are not to be measured simply in terms of the hours at work in the week, even though that is a simple measure of the private time displaced by our work. As we struggle together to meet the several demands upon us, but increasingly slip behind with our various projects, working relationships tend to deteriorate, and a variety of other factors increase levels of conflict and stress. (We reviewed some of the factors in Chapter 2.) It is a straw that breaks the camel's back; the immediate cause of breakdown (a total log-jam of work, or a sudden and disabling illness) may have been some quite minor element that was added to an existing pile of demands and concerns.

Readers will set their own personal limits to what is acceptable. If they already feel that their workloads are excessive in those terms, the problem may be that of 'breaking out' of the spiral – of escaping from the treadmill

– and we have made suggestions about doing that in Chapter 3. The issue of setting maximum limits to workloads opens into wider social issues. Long working weeks and years are a feature of contemporary life for those gainfully and legally employed in the United Kingdom and other 'advanced' economies. They are attended by a variety of social ills that can readily be connected, directly or indirectly, with the displacement by excessive workloads of non-work activities of all kinds, including some that form important threads in the fabric of a healthy society. Whether or not you are already at the end of your tether, what can be seen is that if the 'workload drivers' – the factors that increase the demands upon us – are not attacked, they are all too likely to extend workloads without limit, so that the outer bounds of the sustainable will most certainly be reached, and forms of individual and systemic breakdown will become widespread.

In thinking about these matters it is useful to retain a sense of the complexity of the factors that raise the individual and personal cost of demands in the workplace. We need to allow for the difference between the *demands* placed upon us, and the *supply* of time and effort we provide to meet those demands. By saying 'no' we reject a demand; by saying 'not so much' we seek to reduce the demand. We do this to match our supply (the personal cost to ourselves) better to the totality of demands.

We can use here the contrast between the quantity of work demanded of us; the quality of work demanded of us; and our own efficiency in producing work of a given quality (cf. the NSS model that we introduced in Chapter 3). We can reduce the personal cost (in time and effort) of our workload by:

- becoming more efficient (increasing our speed of working on particular tasks); or

- compromising on quality (by reducing the standards we set for adequate completion of a task); or

- reducing the demands (the number of tasks we undertake in the first place).

Becoming more efficient, wherever we can, is both important and helpful. But we accept that, on its own, it is most unlikely to solve all our workload problems. We need, somehow or other, to reduce the total demands upon us, whether by some quantitative change in the 'workload-drivers'; or by lowering our standards. In the United Kingdom there are debates raging around these issues as we write. As outer limits of personal production are reached, and distracting pressures in working groups build up, quality will inevitably be reduced, unless the quantitative aspects are addressed. (The discussion about class size in schools, which finds an echo also in some commentary about staff-student ratios and contact hours in universities, is an example of a discussion about the effect of quantitative factors on quality, in this case, the quality of learning.)

Stemming the flood of demands

What we *can* do for ourselves is to understand as well as we are able, by observing how we work, and what our own limits seem to be, what we can reasonably do; and to negotiate with the appropriate authority to contain our workloads within those limits. This is a non-trivial task, as we noted above, because we have so many 'customers': within our own universities, in our research and professional communities, and in the wider academic world.

In many areas of work, the campaign to reduce demand will of necessity go beyond the individual. At the departmental level, as we have indicated in Chapter 9, we can campaign for agreed systems for distributing work so that at least we each have a fair share of the work to be done. A useful side-effect of adopting such systems is that colleagues are apt to become more conscious of the time- and effort-costs of various jobs. We can seek to ensure that as new procedures are introduced and old ones modified, they are minimally costly of time and effort. Where time-costs have in the past been ignored, such attention should yield useful benefits.

In many areas of academic work (such as research) and in initiatives involving kinds of work of which we have little experience, it may prove very hard to *estimate* time-costs before the event. But making an attempt to work out the likely range of costs may well pay off handsomely.

Example: developing new computer-based materials for teaching.

In recent years, by local initiative but also in the context of some major national programmes, many colleagues have been involved in developing new teaching materials ('courseware') for delivery to students on computers and computer networks. By now, there are many documented cases of projects in this area, and there are figures available estimating (for example) the likely ratio of development time to student contact time when using some standard 'high-level' courseware-development tools. Most British universities have staff who have been involved in producing courseware; and much more has been abandoned or superseded than is currently in use. Anyone attracted by the idea of 'computerising' some part of their teaching would do well to seek out others with experience, and to listen to their tales of woe. (In addition to local sources of information, there are the CTI (Computers in Teaching Initiative) centres in the United Kingdom that support development and dissemination of courseware in particular disciplinary areas, and can put teachers in touch with staff of other universities who may have relevant experience.)

Computing is an area of rapid change; and of a cut-throat market place. Universities are significant purchasers of hardware and of software and 'software tools' including some programs that are marketed as making courseware development easy and painless. We do well to remember that our believing such sales talk makes somebody else some money, and to be cautious before concluding that the use of this or that development tool will be easy and quick.

Moral:

> An investment of time 'researching' the costs of some new activity in support of research or teaching, is worthwhile and can give us a realistic notion of the likely time-costs should we decide to start on this new activity.

We do not always consider the past costs of similar activity, even when we have experience of it. One reason for 'discounting the future' is that we discount the past: we forget the effort and time it took us to complete a task, and belittle our own past efforts. We set out to do a similar thing, expecting it to be quick and easy. What we can expect is that as time-factors increasingly enter into our decision-making, a better understanding of the costs of what we seek to do will permeate our thinking. This should help to forestall 'burn-out' or a painful breakdown. We offer three strategies for containing total workload:

(1) the self-renewing workload;

(2) the resource-driven approach;

(3) working towards a sensible division of labour.

The 'self-renewing' workload

We take this title from a proposal of a national committee on library provision that university libraries should become 'self-renewing'. This was bureaucratic 'newspeak' for limiting the book-space and discarding as many books as were newly purchased. The idea that such a proposal might be made for research libraries seemed, then as it does now, a serious abandonment of principles. But if there had been an absolute limit on bookspace, such a course would have been inevitable. There *is* an absolute limit on our time and effort. As and when it is reached, there will be no new books in our personal work libraries that do not displace old activities. There will be no new tasks, no additions to student numbers, no new procedures, that do not displace some old ones, or reduce the effort spent on them. Even if in some nooks and crannies of our departments and research units there is scope for more work to be done, sooner or later we shall have to learn to live within the maxima. So why not start now?

How do we start? by insisting, when any new imposition is laid upon us, that a compensating reduction is made in the existing commitments. In this way we achieve the 'self-renewing workload'. A habit of enforcing the self-renewing workload should engender a respect for the costs in time and effort of the various impositions that are placed upon us, or that we place upon ourselves.

The resource-driven approach

In financial budgeting, we constrain our plans to our resources. This point is especially poignant in contemporary United Kingdom universities, which are held to very tight budgetary targets by funding councils (guided by government). Universities are not permitted to make financial losses year after year, on pain of being 'taken over' and managed by accountants (if not of being closed or merged with other institutions); they cannot make substantial profits either, at least from that part of their income that comes from the public purse. *If only* we were able to manage our time as we manage our money; and to make a virtue of cutting our coat to suit our cloth; then indeed we could live within our means. To be sure, we live in a competitive world. The situation for universities is like that of the United Kingdom at the 1996 Olympics: matched against the world's best, but with a diminishing financial and educational base on which to found the development of world-class performers, in a field where only world class counts. But we do well to remember that world class can also kill or maim, where individuals are forced beyond their personal resources (as has happened, for example, with some former teenage gymnasts). In such cases, 'living within your means' is a condition of any continued living at all, short of irreversible disablement. Choices may well be made for us at 'system' level: a selection of some universities as 'research' institutions, others as mainly teaching institutions. We beg leave to doubt that, even then, the resourcing – at least from government sources – would be sufficient to support the intended ends. Hard decisions may still be needed, but they are also needed now. The resource-limited approach says: live within your income. Thus, as the time-costs of activities become better known, we should strive to contain total activity within a reasonable working week and working year. Pruning ambition is likely to be the price to be paid for the long-term health of the institution, as much as it is the price of long-term health for us as individual academics working in it.

Those of our colleagues who do consultancy work, and members of other professions (such as solicitors and architects) usually record and cost their own time and are able to charge accordingly. Now that our own time is so precious, and in such demand (from so many tasks) we need to develop similar habits ourselves.

Towards a sensible division of labour

In our day-to-day work in departments and research teams, most academics suffer some *imbalances*; the most familiar being an undesired bias of the workload towards administration. As individuals we can seek to manage our time so that we undertake each activity at the best time for it. This is a one-person version of the division of labour. We match the task to the time of day that best fits it. Among our colleagues, most will have competence in teaching, in research, and in administration, but most of them will also have strengths and weaknesses across these areas of work. Some are more effective as teachers; some are more effective in research. Some are excellent administrators.

For historical and financial reasons, the ratio of non-academic support staff – secretarial, administrative and technical staff – to staff whose primary responsibilities and training are for research and teaching, are low in universities, when compared with many other professions and workplaces.

As a result, we do more administrative and clerical work, often not very competently, than our opposite numbers in those other professions. A 'model' department of (say) ten academic staff and one and a half clerical staff might well become more effective overall, in the research productivity of its members as well as the effectiveness in teaching, if it were to move to being a department with eight academic staff and four secretaries. Under the (highly constraining) rules in the 1990s for research funding in United Kingdom universities, such a change would reduce the income of the department, even if its effectiveness were increased. Obviously departments and universities should be free to arrange their staffing mix in order to optimize their performance against the genuine requirements of student learning and excellence in research, without distorting those to meet arbitrary rules on funding that conflict with good management. Let us hope that university authorities will realize this and lobby the funding agencies for a change in the rules.

Why it is so difficult

It is a very difficult thing to change your own behaviour to become (even) more productive, especially if you are already sprinting to keep up. It is even harder to undertake the kind of re-negotiation and campaigning – involving others at departmental and university levels, and in our trade unions – to contain and to reduce workloads at their source. We may need to recognize that *some* of the reasons why we find it difficult to do such things lie within ourselves, acting alone or in concert with our academic colleagues. We close this chapter by reviewing those factors.

In Chapter 2 we listed a number of factors in the world around us that tend to raise and to complicate our workloads: to present us with ever more pressing challenges to manage our own working time. As we have seen in many different ways by now, the problem of managing time results from a complex interaction of such external demands and pressures with aspects of our own responses: our acquired skills and competences, our motives and values, our beliefs.

In order to reduce total demand to manageable proportions, we need to attend both to the external sources that produce the demand, and to our own response to demands – to the reasons why (hitherto) we may have found it difficult or impossible to say 'no' to extra impositions. There will be many individual differences – some colleagues are simply more ambitious for fame and glory than are others, some are more driven by a need to solve a research problem, or to bring their students to understand some particular subject-matter, than are others. But we think we can detect some common traits of academics and some common habits of academic decision-making that produce a resistance to any tactics designed to reduce workloads. We hope that by setting them out, we will make it easier for you to detect and to defuse them.

Collegiality

The 'college' is our model of the academic community: a club of scholars who manage all their own affairs. We think of this as the privilege of ancient universities, but something of the college existed in younger universities that began life as clubs of professors. By today all these universities have become large corporations with many thousands of students. They have come, in many respects, to resemble other large corporations, with elements of 'line-management': *hierarchical* structures with commands being sent down from one level of the hierarchy to the next. Becher and Kogan (1980) document the interplay of the collegial and hierarchical aspects of modern university life.

What we seem to have is a *confusion* between the two structures: sometimes we think of ourselves, among our academic colleagues, in the collegial mode, as peers and equals, empowered to make decisions among our own group; at other times, when commands come down from above, we tend to react in hierarchical mode, passing the commands down the line, expecting unquestioning obedience. The confusion is compounded when, as is commonly the case, 'above' is a place populated by other (senior) academics, who form the membership of senates, and central university committees, or who have become senior executive officers of universities or of national funding councils. It is common human psychology to accept requests from trusted colleagues for whom already we may have done some smaller service (Cialdini, 1993).

Collegiality neuters resistance to new impositions through the sense that the officer giving the order is 'one of us'; we may find it hard to keep a distance from it and to resist it. Within our local group, resistance involves entering into conflict; it is seen as aggressive rather than as an assertion of rights, so the group lapses into passivity. But passivity against an imposition involves an acceptance of new work – more activity. As this process repeats itself, and colleagues become more and more weighed down, the cost of resistance is felt to be even more unacceptable.

The response to this is to be assertive. Claim collegial rights against those who request us to perform extra duties: ask for good reasons, and for due recompense. If these are denied, reflect that collegiality that is not reciprocated is undermined. The officer whom you took for a colleague is revealed as a (would-be) line-manager and should be treated accordingly.

Subject, service – and self

The 'workload-drivers' that are for ever on the increase, such as student numbers, and demands for publication, and administrative impositions, present us with imperatives. We have just seen how some social and institutional factors may make it extremely difficult for us to reject the next such imperative. Other factors derive from the particular content of those imperatives. Case by case, they may evoke in us some elements of personal ambition, or of commitment to our academic discipline and also to public service.

Subject

A contemporary academic has usually been pursuing his or her subject for at least six years, full-time, before gaining a first university appointment as a lecturer. It is likely that the commitment to the subject was developed earlier, perhaps many years earlier. Research and teaching is undertaken not out of external necessity, but out of a wish to pursue the subject and to enthuse others in it.

We want to discover the truth, to defend the truths we have discovered against criticism. So when we have an idea for a new theory, we think nothing of working late to sketch out the details. Academics are just the people who are motivated to burn the midnight oil in working out the new proof, the new interpretation. They are the 'creative artists' of the intellectual world. So too when a critical article purporting to refute the central argument of one of our books appears in a leading journal, we do not think of the time-cost of writing the rebuttal. And when others exhibit ignorance of our subject, or when we are in a position to initiate fresh young minds into it, the subject is our calling, and we feel strongly the urge to enlighten them. We betray our calling if we turn away from them.

A new opportunity to conduct research, to read a paper, to reach new students with our ideas, latches on to our subject-commitment.

Service

The larger world that we survey from our subject-interest is mostly ignorant of quite basic facts and principles that they clearly need. If friends, or anyone seeking advice, approaches us as a subject expert, we feel the need to oblige them, in the name of the subject and of the truth. Our devotion to the subject and its advancement is compatible with a role as latter-day sages in the global information village. (This phenomenon can be illustrated from the conversations one can now read on the Internet as scholars put and answer questions worldwide. Not to mention the role of subject-experts as talking heads on educational television programmes; and in popular science writing in the quality press.) For those of us with a professional service to offer – doctors, applied scientists, lawyers – there is a separate, and remunerated, service role. But our main point is that any academic as subject-practitioner (first and foremost) feels a duty to respond to requests for 'services' that call upon their expertise.

Our disposition to respond to invitations to add to our workloads by performing tasks related to our own research area is reinforced by the sense that our own expertise is *unique*, a feature that we have already remarked upon in Chapter 2.

Self

Many academics are ambitious, most would like to progress up the promotional ladder during their careers. When new demands come in, they may offer opportunities for personal advancement, or for improving one's curriculum vitae with a view to promotion. If 'macho' attitudes to workloads are common among our seniors – the colleagues who will be writing our references – we may feel obliged to accept new impositions in order to satisfy them. There is a powerful mechanism at work here. Heads of department and other officers who combine a managerial responsibility with the opportunity to recommend anyone for promotion have a vested interest in valuing and rewarding a disposition in colleagues to accept sacrificial work-levels, since it enables them to delegate new tasks that are imposed upon their workgroups – tasks that they might otherwise have to undertake themselves. A crash course in resisting such invitations can be obtained by reading Blanchard *et al.* (1990).

The response to this is to become stoical about your limitations. Reflect that, however much you do, it will be only .001 per cent of what you would like to have done, given the time. Conclude that the difference between alternative 1: .001 per cent with burn-out, and alternative 2: .0005 per cent and a reasonable and sustainable quality of life, is not significant – *and* you live longer under alternative 2!

Competition

It is a commonplace that life in contemporary western economies is competitive. In the experience of all who have enjoyed schooling and some exposure to organized sporting activity, there are two areas of life where competition dominates: sport, and academic work. For all of us, schoolwork involved competition, most obviously in the competition for grades in public examinations. Academics are among the individuals who took to this competition, and thrived in it. Habits formed throughout 15-20 years of schooling and undergraduate study are well-ingrained by the time an academic takes up a first appointment.

Work in universities provides many opportunities for competition: for promotion; for research grants; for publication space in leading journals. Individuals who are competitive are motivated to join whatever competitions there are on offer.

An excellent way of getting most academics to work harder is to tell them that they are competing for some particular prize or ranking. In the increasingly 'market'-oriented academic world, competitions abound, and workloads increase.

Your response to this should be to say 'pass'! Think twice before entering the next competition. Notice the trick that is being played on you when someone says: 'look, department x (or colleague y) is pulling ahead of you'.

The treadmill effect

New impositions flow in. All too often, like viruses, they attach themselves to 'host' mechanisms that make them more destructive: our ambitions, our prior commitments to people or subjects, our automatic response to invitations to join competitions. All it takes to counteract these forces is a reflective understanding of what is happening. But another factor militates against that: the sheer pace of activity, driven by day-to-day and minute-to-minute events that call for some immediate action. *Of course* we shall take stock … but after finishing this pile of marking, and getting that report (due last week) completed!

We recognize the difficulty of stopping the world however much you need to get off. That was why we placed 'breaking out' so high on our own agenda for you.

The response to this: Read Chapter 3 again!

Summary of Chapter 10

In this chapter we have considered techniques that you can apply to prevent overload and to help maintain a healthy and fulfilling life. Proposals for stopping the flood of demands on our time have been considered.

---

11   Master of Time

In the introduction to this book we promised that at the completion of the course you could award yourself a 'Master of Time'. We have now come to the moment of truth.

This chapter has two purposes. First, it is a summary and aide-mémoire for you, stressing the important points that go before and extending them with some conventional time management words of wisdom. Second, as you go through this chapter you should consider the following criteria for the award of a Master's degree, which have been adapted from those for the more conventional university subject areas, to discover how much you have achieved.

Five essential criteria for a 'Master of Time'

A 'Master of Time' should be awarded to someone who

(1) has critically investigated and evaluated the topic of time and self management;

(2) understands the research methods appropriate to the subject area;

(3) has shown evidence of improvement and proficiency in handling time;

(4) has shown initiative and independence of thought in the use of time;

(5) has made a distinct contribution to the subject area.

Being in this case your own examiner *you* must decide if you fulfil the necessary criteria. If you decide that you do, then award yourself a 'Master of Time' but remember that such a degree is only the beginning. You will now be in a position to do further research in this area and hopefully will be able to keep 'time' more or less under your own control from now on.

Notes on the criteria

Here are some notes to help you to decide that you have successfully fulfilled the five criteria.

(1) Have you investigated and evaluated critically the topic of time and time management?

When you have completed the first ten chapters in this book and have carried out the research and exercises suggested then you have fulfilled the first criterion.

(2) Do you understand the research methods appropriate to the subject area?

Chapter 3 contains a nine-step research plan together with four models for viewing the problem. Now that you have successfully completed the course you should have ideas on methods that could be applied to the subject of time and self management and begin to apply them to your work and indeed to your lifestyle.

(3) Have you shown evidence of improvement and proficiency in handling time?

In the sections that follow we have cast the main points on time management in the form of questions taken either from the text or from conventional time management wisdom. In particular if you have shown proficiency in handling time the questions following the section on personal time management should be answered with 'yes'.

Having a large number of 'yes' answers will provide you with the evidence that you have become more proficient.

If you have answered 'no' to a number of questions, then you need to explore these questions in your mind and determine if you need to take any further action with regard to them. Only you will know if you have really improved. See also criterion (4) below.

(4) Have you shown initiative and independence of thought in respect of the use of time?

Are you are at the point where you have begun to take what we have given you and are adapting it to your own needs and purposes? If so, then you have fulfilled this criterion.

(5) Have you made a distinctive contribution to the subject area?

We have guided you to the best of our ability, but the joy in being a teacher is that your student outgrows you. Write to us at the publisher's address, given at the beginning of the book, and let us know how we can add to and improve the next edition of this book. If we are able to use your suggestion we will acknowledge your help in the next edition. In this way you will have made a distinctive contribution to the subject area.

The remainder of this chapter concentrates on the following areas to enhance your strategies for time management:

■ Working with others

   (a) research

   (b) teaching and learning

   (c) administrative tasks and planning

   (d) developing good working relationships

   (e) possible courses of action

■ Paper work

(a) organising and retrieving it

(b) writing

(c) reading

■ Personal time management

(a) sustain and improve your performance

(b) give yourself time to reflect

Working with others

One of the principal reasons for good time management is to free up time for the creative, reflective and personal aspects of research that cannot always be quantified in terms of time.

Research

Time management can be applied to routine tasks but much of our research work is non-routine and being tried for the first time.

Assuming that you plan to allot a specific period of time to your research then you must contain this in your total workload and defend the space you have made against all comers. Strategies for containing total workload are:

■ The 'self-renewing' workload

■ Striving for a sensible division of labour

The self-renewing workload

Are you trying to achieve the 'self-renewing' workload?

We should strive to contain our total activity within a reasonable working week and year to allow us to protect both our working and our research time. It should also ensure both the long-term health of the institution and our own long-term health as individual academics who work within it.

Insist, when any new imposition is laid on you, that a compensating re-duction is made in existing commitments. Thus we achieve the 'self-renewing workload'. Developing the habit of enforcing this should engender a respect for the costs in time and effort of the various impositions which are placed upon us, or that we place upon ourselves. Remember to include the required amount of research time within the total.

Sensible division of labour

Have you discussed possible collaborations which use the strengths of your-self and colleagues for the advantage of your group?

We must now count the cost in time and effort of our plans and projects. Of our colleagues, most will have competence in teaching, in research, and in administration, but there will also be many who will have strengths and weaknesses right across these areas of work. We need to collaborate with colleagues to make the best use of everyone's strengths for the benefit of all and for the benefit of us as individuals.

We also need to recognise that the most careful plans are apt to fail, where tasks take longer than expected, or new demands supervene. We need therefore to develop juggling skills, that is, to find various ways of keeping the threads of numerous tasks in hand, and to learn to bounce back from interruptions.

Above all, if time for research is one of your personal time management goals, use these strategies to guard your research time and not let it be eroded by other things.

Teaching and learning

There are two approaches one can take to teaching and learning:

(1) A conservative approach

   Leave existing methods in place, but seek to reduce time costs of each element (for example, abolish double marking).

(2) A more radical approach

   Replace teaching by tutoring to guide and support students in the use of the learning resources provided for them.

Administrative tasks and planning

Administration covers at least four different types of activity:

(1) Routine tasks within teaching and research

(2) Tasks or roles outside teaching and research

(3) Routine or occasional tasks, for example, departmental meetings, personnel roles, etc.

(4) The work of professional administrators

When we consider administrative activities, what is it that actually takes up our time? Here are some of them:

Receiving, holding, and storing documents

Responding to direct approaches (in person or on the phone)

Arranging, attending or conducting meetings or interviews

Reading forms, reports, memoranda, or committee papers

Obtaining information

Imposing a structure on information, and performing queries or calculations with it

Checking data, evaluating, assessing or scoring performances or records

Making decisions (whether by yourself or in concert with others)

Writing memoranda, letters, reports, minutes

The ways of reducing the time demands of administration are by lessening the time taken up by individual administration tasks; cutting out whole tasks; or harmonizing the demands of all your projects and roles.

Do you strive to reduce the time taken up by administrative tasks? Here are some candidates for surgery:

some committees

monitoring activities

documentation and information systems involving duplication

maintaining archives and audit trails

organisational structures in which activities are duplicated

Developing good working relationships

Is your attitude towards colleagues one of trust, and do they show themselves to be worthy of that trust? Can we get other people to help us in our time management control? Equally important, how can we prevent them from hindering us in our efforts? Everything points to the fact that we have to achieve a shared understanding of the importance of time. This may not be very easy, because the habit of treating time as endless dies hard. These are things which should be discussed with any working group with whom you become involved.

Developing relationships is part of our job-relationship with our classes, with our responsibility for other staff, and with our responsibility as heads of departments and leaders of research teams.

If relationships are good, mutual support in time management is a benefit we can enjoy. If sour, effectiveness is challenged, control of time is derailed. Our capacity to control our emotions and manage time is affected by the atmosphere in which we work.

The moral is clear: spend time developing good working relationships. Time spent on developing and sustaining relationships is time well invested. Ignoring them is perilous even if it appears to save time in the short run.

Trusting colleagues

The character of our working relationships, of all our personal relationships, has a pervasive effect on time.

If we have trust in our colleagues – to keep their promises or do a job well – we will be happier to ask them to undertake some task for us, thus lightening our own load. Hostility between two colleagues always threatens effectiveness of collaboration and with it mutual scope for time management.

Good teamwork

A basic element in good management is to count the cost of any new activity, and to assign adequate resources to it. Time is a strictly limited resource.

The value of time should become a common concern for your working group. One way of putting it on the group's agenda is to arrange a short time management course attended by all staff in the particular group.

Good teamwork and effective distribution of tasks in a working group require that as far as possible jobs should be done by people who are able to do them with least effort. What can be done to help achieve good teamwork? Collaborating with others will achieve economies of scale, for example, not interrupting others unnecessarily, giving good notice of intent. Good teamwork also requires that individuals who are better than others at tasks needed by the whole group are rewarded and recognised for their contribution to the whole work of the group. The late 1990s funding environment of the United Kingdom universities militated against a rational distribution of labour.

Possible courses of action

A feature of the increasing pace of academic life is that more and more forms and reports are required with ever shorter deadlines. Increased stress and reduced efficiency of time-use make planning more difficult and tend to introduce interruptions which reduce your overall effectiveness and raise the total time-cost of the activities they have interrupted.

Meeting deadlines

If deadlines are not met someone has to chase. It is sometimes necessary to chase up replies because we have had no acknowledgement of the original request. Minimal acknowledgement by e-mail or pre-printed card can save time all round.

Being punctual

Simple punctuality saves time. If you are part of a *quorum* the time of those who arrive on time will not be used to best effect as they wait for you.

Arranging helpful timetables

As individuals we should seek to negotiate with those preparing the timetables schedules that enable us to make the best use of our time. This may mean bunching teaching commitments to free time for preparation, marking and research without frequent changes of gear into the teaching mode, or having to clear working areas repeatedly for student use.

Delegating tasks

It is unnecessary to spend time in making decisions about those things which can be delegated to others working with or for you. You need both to train and trust those people. The crucial questions to ask yourself about these tasks should be:

What am I doing that others could do? and

Do I delegate these tasks when possible and appropriate?

Personal aspects

There are certain skills or attitudes which you must have if you are to work well with others. One of the essentials is a sensitivity to their needs as well as to your own. You should ask yourself the following:

Do you respect the importance of other people's time as well as your own?

Do you praise rather than blame?

Do you make life pleasant both for yourself and others?

Meetings

Meetings are an accepted part of academic life but as soon as two or more people are gathered together to perform some task the total time cost rises. As time is increasingly pressured, it should be increasingly valued. We need to be very sure that meetings are needed and that meeting time is well used. Here is a checklist of points that should help you to achieve this:

Meetings you go to:

- Keep the number of meetings you attend to a minimum.

- Limit the time in a meeting by going only to the relevant part.

- Use non-productive time in meetings for planning/timetabling and so on.

- Prepare for the meeting beforehand. This means that you can be more informed and focused in the meeting.

Meetings you are in control of:

- For all meetings you hold have a written agenda which clearly states what decisions have to be taken.

- Start and finish on time – keep meetings short.

- Only ask people essential to the meeting to attend.

- Keep things moving.

- Keep your comments brief and to the point.

- Make sure the minutes of the meeting has an action list naming people.

Meetings with individuals:

- Meet in *their* office so that you can leave when you want to.

- If in your office, stand up to greet your visitor and stay standing up – if you invite them to sit down it will lengthen the meeting.

- Make sure your meeting is not interrupted – you can get someone to interrupt if they stay too long.

Planning
The following list should help you to plan ahead:

- Prioritize your tasks but set a balance between the urgent ones and those that are important to you.

- Plan ahead, making a yearly/monthly/weekly plan; but be flexible, do not expect life to work that way. The reason for having a plan is to know where you are going so that you can act, which is preferable to putting things off.

- Regularly revise your plan.

- Reserve time for yourself each day: to do research; to think; to read.

- Make an outline plan for each day – be pleased if you achieve 50 per cent of that plan.

- Break complex and large tasks down into simpler ones which you can achieve and show progress on.

- Keep a notebook or electronic organiser to record your ideas, names, notes of meetings, etc.

- Try to finish the job on hand before going on to the next, but also recognize that in reality you may have to juggle several things at once.

Decisions

You must recognize that it is very difficult to get all the facts before making a decision. Try to define the problem as clearly as possible by collecting all the information you can. Then having reviewed the best and worst scenario, make your decision. Do not take too much time over making a decision, nor use too much energy on unimportant decisions. And most important, do not worry after you have made the decision; if you must worry, do it before you make the decision. Remember that afterwards it is too late!

Where possible, get people to give you solutions, not problems. In this way you are training those around you to become decision-makers. (Their abilities are developed and the load is taken off your shoulders.) If you make a wrong decision, analyse what went wrong so that you can prevent it from happening next time.

Paper work

To keep up with the heavy flows of paper into our working spaces we need to give some time to designing and using systems for controlling and storing paper documents. A few common-sense principles that respect the physical form of these documents, and our own needs in storing them, will go a long way towards dealing with the paper problem.

Recording and storing information takes (someone's) time and effort in creating and maintaining the storage system. The ideal is to keep needed information in a single but secure copy that is readily accessible to all who may want to find it.

Traditional paper storage methods do not make the ideal easy to achieve, not for reasonable time and effort. Electronic methods do hold up some hope of economy in storage with ease of access.

Organising and retrieving paperwork

Academics are prime producers of paper: articles, books, lecture notes, mark sheets, reports on students, applications for research grants, promotion applications. Organizing, storing and retrieving them efficiently is essential.

The following lists some of the basic considerations in dealing with the organization and retrieval of paperwork:

- Physical considerations

  These depend on shape, size, rigidity (or lack of) of documents.

- Functions of card containers

  These are to hold floppy papers so they do not bend over or fall; to hold grouped related papers together; to provide a title area; to permit random access to individual documents and guarantee their return to same place in the sequence.

- Conceptual constraints

  There is no right way of classifying documents in order to put them in files. Categories employed to group papers should be usable both for grouping papers, sorting new papers and for finding and refiling old ones. Most categories grow naturally from the subject matter you are dealing with.

■ Practical principles

You should have files not piles. Type of files available include:

box files

filing cabinets with hanging drawers

rotary systems

lateral shelf-filing systems

We recommend you think of files like books. We find familiar books on our shelves more quickly because we know what they look like and because there is variety in colours and styles.

An alterative to the filing cabinet is the filing shelf. Box files mimic books but may be too high for many bookshelves and take up same volume of space for one or a hundred sheets of paper. A mixture of filing cabinets and boxes is a good idea as it gives variety and distinction. Some labelling systems offer a variety of colours to help lend files individuality.

Flexibility is something to consider in a filing system. Ease of adding another file, ease of titling, re-titling is something to watch.

■ Computer-assisted paper management

E-mail has displaced paper correspondence for many purposes but some people still feel the need to print the messages out. When documents are received, created or stored on computers, document management problems for computer users are similar to the paper management problems we have been discussing.

There may be help in using a computer program. A computer might be used to create and hold a catalogue of file titles, an index of documents, a list of tasks and associated documents. Lists are to the computer text files or database tables. Lists can be stored in the simplest of computers with advantages of editing and searching. Installing and learning a new computer application is itself costly in time.

Processing paper documents

We control a flow of papers across our desk; these should have designated locations:

your working area

the appropriate file

the waste paper basket

the 'out tray' or post box

To retain several documents for current attention create special holding areas. But do not allow current papers to accumulate in such a way that they are not dealt with promptly or lose their identity in anonymous piles. You can keep a tickler file numbered for each day of the month, with items in each day's slot that you plan to deal with on that day.

If it happens that there is an imbalance in your system, deal with it by spending more time in sorting and dealing with new papers, discarding more of them or placing them directly into files; or spend less time on individual items; or spend more time directly at your desk dealing with working papers.

Papers held back for action for several days should go into the main filing system but there ought to be a note of the relevant task and place of filing on your agenda list.

In general a document landing on your desk for consideration attaches itself to one or another topic and invites distinct action from you:

reply directly;

decide on opinion;

get information or opinion of others;

read (this is for longer documents that need extra time);

hold for next committee meeting.

Set out below are three valuable tips on good practice for processing paper documents.

(1) Deal with your post/e-mail every day to avoid overload.

(2) Have only *one* job on your desk at any one time. Keep the rest in your filing system, in-tray etc. until you can spend time on it.

(3) Clear your desk before you leave at night.

Writing

Before you begin to write anything, ask yourself whether it is necessary to write it at all. When you do have to write, keep your letters, reports and memos short and to the point. If you have to write the same type of letter over and over again, it is a good idea to create a standard letter on your computer. Below are some useful points to remember:

- Keep copies of everything you write – the original may get lost.

- If you do not have keyboard skills, acquire them.

- Practise clear and legible handwriting; in these days of computers a clear handwritten note can carry a lot of weight.

Reading

Think what you are reading for. Be prepared to skim, use indexes, tables of contents, cribs (summaries and reviews). Some note, however brief, should be kept in your project diary of what has been looked at. Highlight key sentences/phrases in your own book (never a library book) – or a photocopy. Always bear in mind that reading and writing are forms of thinking; ask yourself what you are trying to achieve and try to keep the main question in mind as you read. This will save precious time.

Personal time management

By now you should have some ideas on your strengths and weaknesses concerning time management. This section reiterates what has been discussed in earlier chapters. See how you measure up now. There are four key questions which you should consider:

(1) Are you clear in your mind what it is that matters to you?

(2) Do you do all you can to reduce your stress, tension and anxiety?

(3) Do you realise that time management is self management?

(4) Do you know yourself? (The following sections will help you with this.)

As we discussed in Chapter 3, the key aims above have to be kept in view if we are to master our time.

Sustain and improve your performance

Remember that 'yes' is the preferred answer to these questions and all those that follow.

(1) Do you want to break out of the spiral?

(2) You must not be discouraged by your first efforts. Do you keep trying?

(3) Do you sustain your efforts until the desired result is attained?

(4) Do you find that you can now achieve what you set out to achieve?

Give yourself time to reflect

Bear in mind that creative ideas, research and problem-solving do not conform to strict timetables. Therefore, it is necessary to carve time out of an already overloaded schedule in order to be able to research the topic. To achieve control over time, it is a good idea to take out a little each day, first to define the plan of the research and then carry it out one piece at a time, thereby gradually beginning to assume control.

Your personal action-research model needs to provide a place for the notion of progress along a continuum, using an iterative process; not just the notion of (one-off) achievement. This idea – the move from focus on product to focus on process informs many of our suggestions. The kinds of problems that you are facing are so daunting to you that a once-for-all solution is not likely to be immediately available. A gradual build-up is required.

Personal morale is much improved if you are able to characterize the problem in such a way that you can see your response is getting better. Here are some personal time management tips:

- Know when you work best and use that time for creative rather than routine tasks.

- Keep a time diary – practise estimating time for each task.

- Prioritize your tasks, then concentrate fully on one thing at a time.

- Make sure that you get enough sleep, eat sensibly and take care with your health.

- Conserve your energy where possible.

- Learn to relax, especially in your breaks.

- Listen to your mind, and your body.

- Set aside time for your own use.

- Do jobs right first time.

- Set performance standards for yourself.

- Try to avoid being behind with your work.

- Do not ask too much of yourself.

- Accept what cannot be changed.

- Do not worry excessively about what people will think of you.

The need to say 'no'

To take control of both our time and our work, and to stay in control once we have regained it, we need to be able to contain the total demands on our time. For an academic saying 'no' is sometimes an easy matter, but more often, it is somewhere between difficult and quite impossible. Do you recognise that you will never have enough time? If the demands on us rise without limit, then clearly something will give way.

Remember each of us is subject to a personal upper limit beyond which any attempt to do more will be counterproductive and beyond this limit our productivity will drop. We have a right to a private life, to a family life, to some waking time on personal projects – and so a right to limit our total working time in such a way as to allow for these activities. We have a right to health – and so a right to contain the stresses and demands of work to ensure that our health is not threatened.

Many academics are ambitious, most would like to progress up the promotional ladder. Anyone in a managerial capacity has a vested interest in valuing and rewarding a disposition in colleagues to accept sacrificial levels of work load. Become stoical about your limitations. Reflect that, however much you do, it will only be a very small amount of what you would have done if you had time. The difference between working to burnout and having a reasonable and sustainable quality of life is not significant yet the latter is far more preferable.

The characteristics of a 'Master of Time'

How did you rate yourself on the five criteria given at the beginning of this chapter? Here are some final words of wisdom that may help.

A problem that is being worked on is being managed, that is, as soon as you feel that you are understanding and engaging with the problem, then the personal threat that it presents is already much reduced.

Goals are needed to inform short-term plans; they express the values we care about. At every stage we need a clear long-term vision that informs our medium and short-term goals. Should the last set of short-term plans fail, we go back to the drawing board and modify our plan, modifying some of the goals, abandoning others. The goals are like the carrot dangling just out of reach that gets us moving forward. As we move forward it recedes. No matter as long as we are moving forward.

The best thing to change first is something that yields a good benefit at low cost. Effort should not be dispersed on too wide a front; as soon as one finds something significant it is best to concentrate on that aspect of the work. Even without the help of such a model, you can and should choose to focus on a single area of change – an area of maximum gain, where a first move can be completed quickly and can be expected to make a difference that matters to you. No one can do more than one thing at a time.

As with most undertakings, the success of an experiment depends largely on the care taken with preliminary preparations and the care with which it is carried out. Treat time management research in this way and it will succeed for you. Do not try to change everything at once. Regard time management as a voyage of discovery; as a research project that you can undertake yourself without additional funding.

In contemporary Western economies life is competitive and work in universities provides many opportunities for competition – for promotion, for research grants, for publication space in leading journals. An excellent way to get most academics to work harder is to tell them that they are competing for some prize or ranking. Your response should be: think twice before entering the next competition. Notice the trick being played upon you when someone says 'Look, department x/colleague y is pulling ahead of you'.

New impositions flow in. All it takes to counteract these forces is a reflective understanding of what is happening. But another factor militates against that – the sheer pace of activity, driven by day-to-day, minute-by-minute events that call for some immediate action. Of course we will take stock … but after finishing this pile of marking, and getting that report (due last week) completed!

What we seem to have is a confusion between two structures: sometimes we think of ourselves among our academic colleagues, in the collegial mode, as peers and equals, empowered to make decisions among our own group. At other times when commands come down from above, we tend to react in hierarchical mode. It is common human psychology to accept requests from trusted colleagues for whom we may have done some smaller service. Collegiality neuters resistance to new impositions through the sense that the 'officer' giving the orders is 'one of us'; we may find it hard to keep a distance from it and resist it.

Your response should be to be assertive. Claim collegial rights against those who request us to perform extra duties: ask for good reasons, and for due recompense. The officer you took for a colleague is revealed as a (would-be) line-manager and should be treated accordingly. In order to reduce total demand to manageable proportions, we need to attend both to the external sources that produce the demand, and our own response to the demands – to the reasons why (hitherto) we may have found it impossible or difficult to say 'no' to extra impositions. There will be many individual differences – some colleagues are simply more ambitious for fame and glory than others, some are driven by the need to solve a research problem, or to bring their students to understand some particular subject matter than others. There are common traits of academics and common habits of academic decision-making producing a resistance to any tactics designed to reduce work loads. By becoming aware of them it will be easier for you to detect and defuse them.

Academics are the 'creative artists' of the intellectual world. When we pursue our calling we do not reckon the time cost. If individuals are allowed to negotiate their workload from year to year with a system that clearly defines total responsibilities of individual members of staff then they can plan their time without fear that additional tasks will be imposed without notice or recommence. If you are someone who needs to move from 'they are piling too much on me' to 'I can control my work', two insights may help you:

(1) One reason for my view of what they are doing to me is my response to what is happening.

(2) I need to understand how I react, not simply in terms of the current task (the 'what'), but in terms of the way I respond to all tasks – my attitudes, skills, coping systems which include planning, scheduling, interruption-restriction systems etc. (the 'how' and the 'why').

We need to distinguish between standards that are:

- relevant and irrelevant

- internal and external

- appropriate and inappropriate

In particular if we are to minimize the time costs of administration we need to ensure that we do not waste time on internal quality that is strictly irrelevant to the outcome.

A final word

Actually two words – **GOOD LUCK!**

Select Bibliography

Becher, Tony and Kogan, Maurice (1980) *Process and Structure in Higher Education*. London: Heinemann.

Beveridge, W.I.B. (1950) *The Art of Scientific Investigation*. London: Heinemann.

Blanchard, K., Oncken, William, Jr. and Burrows, Hal (1990) *The One Minute Manager Meets the Monkey*. Glasgow: Fontana/Collins.

Covey, Stephen, Merrill, Roger and Merrill, Rebecca (1994) *First Things First*. New York: Simon and Schuster.

Cialdini, Robert B. (1993) *Influence: Science and Practice*. New York: Harper Collins.

Field, Trevor (1992) *The Time of Your Life* (CUA Good Practice Series, no. 12). Manchester: Conference of University Administrators.

Fisher, Shirley (1994) *Stress in Academic Life: The Mental Assembly Line*. Buckingham: Society for Research in Higher Education and the Open University Press.

Juniper, Dean (1991) *The Stress Manual: recognize and resolve the processes and results of stress in the professional teacher*. Dereham: Peter Francis Publishers.

Lansdale, Mark (1988) "The psychology of personal information management", *Applied Ergonomics*, 19: 55-66.

Lansdale, Mark (1991) "Remembering about documents: memory for appearance, format and location", *Ergonomics*, 34 (8): 1161-78.

Lansdale, Mark and Edmonds, E. (1992) "Using memory for events in the design of personal filing systems", *International Journal of Man-Machine Studies*, 36 (7): 97-126.

National Committee of Inquiry into Higher Education (Dearing Committee) (1997) *Higher Education in the Learning Society*. London: HMSO.

Richards, J.H. (1987) "Time management – a review", *Work and Stress*, 1 (1): 73-8.

Rock-Evans, Rosemary (1989) *A Simple Introduction to Data and Activity Analysis.* Sutton, Surrey: Computer Weekly Publications.

Servan-Schreiber, Jean-Louis (1989) *The Art of Time.* London: Bloomsbury.

Sutherland, Valerie and Cooper, Cary (1996) *Understanding Stress: a psychological perspective for health professionals.* London: Chapman and Hall.

Thomas, Glyn (1999) "The process of writing a scientific paper" in Philip Hills (ed.) *Publish or Perish.* Dereham: Peter Francis Publishers.

Treacy, Declan (1991) *Clear Your Desk!* London: Random Century.

Warren, Eve and Toll, Caroline (1993) *The Stress Workbook.* London: Nicholas Brealey (in association with The Industrial Society).

Index

U

V

W